Photographing history
MATHEW BRADY

Britannica Bookshelf—Great Lives for Young Americans

Photographing history

MATHEW BRADY

by Manuel Komroff

*Photographs from the Ansco Historical Collection,
the Chicago Historical Society,
and Kean Archives, Philadelphia*

Published by
BRITANNICA BOOKS
a division of
ENCYCLOPAEDIA BRITANNICA, INC., *Chicago*

Permission to quote from the following works has been granted by the copyright holders: Beaumont Newhall, The History of Photograph from 1839 to the Present *(Museum of Modern Art, 1949);* The Diary of President Polk, *edited by Allan Nevins (Longmans, Green and Company, 1929; courtesy of David McKay Co., Inc.); James D. Horan,* Mathew Brady Historian with a Camera *(Crown, 1955); Roy Meredith,* Mr. Lincoln's Camera Man *(Scribner's, 1946); Margaret Leech,* Reveille in Washington, 1860-1865 *(Harper & Row, Publishers), Robert Taft,* Photography and the American Scene A Social History, *1839-1889 (The Macmillan Company, 1938).*

TABLE OF CONTENTS

LIST OF ILLUSTRATIONS

Chapter 1

The Glorious Horizon of History

The Goddess of Fortune never speaks aloud, but in a far-off whisper, as though she were announcing a verdict in a dream. But youth knows when she has spoken, and he understands, he believes, and he marches forward with confidence, hope, and inspiration. He does not know that this Goddess is very fickle. Sometimes she is with you and sometimes she is against you.

Mathew Brady listened to the whisper of the Goddess of Fortune with confidence and hope when as a 16-year-old boy he left his farm birthplace near Lake George, New York, and journeyed to Saratoga Springs. It was not far from home, about 30 miles, but it was the direction he felt the golden wand of the Goddess was pointing. The year was 1839.

Destiny has a strange way of binding odd things together. In 1839 when this young, redheaded son of Irish parents left the farm to seek his fortune, in that very year, across the Atlantic something happened that was to make his fortune. The discovery of photography was announced to the French Academy of Sciences in 1839.

But genial Mathew Brady did not know this as he journeyed to Saratoga Springs, nor did he know that photography was to make his fortune. It took a little time for the Goddess of Fortune to bring photography and Brady together. But step by step she guided him, and in a very few years he became involved in photography and in the colorful history of the United States.

Little is known of Mathew's youth. He was born in the beautiful Adirondack Mountains of poor Irish parents. Most biographers believe that Brady's parents were immigrants, though Brady himself, on one occasion, gave his parents' names as Andrew and Julia and said that both were born in the United States. Such, however, may not have been the fact. Even the exact location of the farm on which Mathew was born is not known. Brady himself said only that it was in Warren County, New York. And he added that he was born "about 1823-24."

Young Mathew grew up knowing many of the veterans of the American Revolution who had fought in those terrible battles around his birthplace. History, important history, was close to him as a boy, and he could not help but feel its presence. Freedom was in the air. His steps were light as he left home. He was filled with ambition to make something of himself, exactly what he did not know. But a strong force impelled him.

Saratoga Springs was the first stopping place as Mathew moved toward the horizon of history. There he apprenticed himself to a casemaker to learn the trade of making cases for watches, for instruments, and for jewelry. Young Mathew was a small youth, only five feet six inches tall, slim, wearing eyeglasses, and inclined to be delicate. He was not robust enough to undertake heavy labor, and since he had little education, he was unable to find better employment.

Casemaking may sound like a very dull trade, but there too Fortune watched over him. His skill in casemaking helped him in a very curious way a few years later to learn many of the secrets of photography. And in the early days photography had many secrets.

At Saratoga Springs, 16-year-old Mathew met a 28-year-old portrait painter, William Page. There was something in Page that Mathew admired. And Page at once recognized in young Brady some rare qualities and a hidden artistic talent.

Page helped Mathew in a number of ways: he encouraged him to draw, he gave him a box of crayons, he spoke to him about such aspects of art as composition, perspective, and draftsmanship. Mathew was eager and quick to learn. Page even gave Mathew some instruction in oil painting and allowed him to come to his studio and watch him at work. All of this instruction proved of great value to Mathew a few years later when he began working in photography.

Page found Mathew a happy, friendly, and good companion; and the two became such good friends that they joined forces and moved on from Saratoga Springs to Albany, where Page got a number of portrait commissions. Mathew, having left his casemaking job, became studio assistant to the artist. He stretched canvases, ground colors, washed brushes, and did all the little odd jobs about the studio. In his spare time, Mathew tried his hand at making careful copies of some of Page's crayon drawings and paintings. But Mathew did not give up casemaking completely. He had his tools and some materials, and from time to time he made cases on special order.

Mathew's meeting with William Page and the friendship that developed from it proved to be the first great step forward for the youth toward that great horizon of American history. The second great step came soon thereafter, again through his good artist friend William Page.

William Page had studied painting at the National Academy of Design in New York City with Samuel Finley Breese Morse, who later was to become famous as the inventor of the telegraph. But at the time Page studied with Morse, he was known only as a painter. Born in Massachusetts of a good family, Morse had gone to England after graduating from Yale and had studied painting there. After returning to the United States, he went

[*12*]

through a period of struggle before he gained recognition as a painter. In 1825, when the old Revolutionary War hero, La Fayette, returned from France on a visit to the United States, Morse was commissioned to paint two portraits of him. In the same year he became a founder and was elected the first president of the National Academy of Design. It was there that Page became a favored pupil.

Morse's scientifically curious mind led him to conduct experiments with chemicals and electricity. In 1827 he had attended lectures at Columbia in electromagnetism. Again Morse went to Europe to paint. While returning to the United States in 1832 on the packet ship *Sully,* the idea of the telegraph came suddenly to Morse's mind. This invention was to bring him back again to France and to introduce him to another new discovery—photography. Slowly the Goddess of Fortune moves her men on the checkerboard of destiny.

Young Mathew learned the main facts about Samuel F.B. Morse from William Page, his former pupil who had become his devoted friend and admirer. From time to time, Page added colorful details.

"And what happened to the electric telegraph?" asked young Brady.

"Well, it is an idea. It is an invention. It is something that Morse feels is almost revolutionary. Imagine a long wire strung from here to there, and over this wire electrical impulses can transmit a message. Imagine such a wire strung from Washington to New York. Then if the President of the United States issued a message, the New York newspapers could have it printed within a few hours."

"But would such a long wire be possible?"

"Morse says it could be strung over poles set in the ground. It would be costly but most useful for quick communication. He is convinced it would work and be a great benefit to mankind."

"Do you understand how it works?" asked Mathew.

"No, not exactly. Except that the current goes through an electromagnet. He showed it to me several times, but I do not have a head for science. Morse has been spending most of his time trying to perfect this invention. His studio is a jumble of wires, bottles, wet batteries, iron bars, magnets, and everything—a jumble of confusion. He has no room for his painting. In fact, I think he's given up painting completely. Of course, he still teaches painting and sculpture at the University of the City of New York. He has to keep his teaching job to pay for his experiments. Two years ago he finished a rough model of the telegraph and applied for a patent. But the invention is so different and so new that the patent office has not, as yet, been able to make up its mind."

"He has been waiting all this time?"

"No. He is not a man to sit around idle. He has his classes at the University, and in his spare time he works at perfecting his invention. Then, some months ago, he left for Europe, where he is now making application for a

French patent. He has already written me twice from Paris. And perhaps I will hear again before he returns."

After a brief silence Page added, "He's a wonderful man, the most wonderful I know. And when he returns I will go down to New York to visit him." Looking intently at young Mathew he added, "And what is more, I will take you with me. It's a promise. You will like Morse and I think he will like you."

Mathew smiled. "Yes, I am sure to like him. I know I will. Once I saw a large engraving made from his allegorical painting, *Dying Hercules*. Oh, that is a man worth knowing."

Page's promise glowed in young Mathew's heart. What would come of such a meeting he did not know, but certainly he felt that something might happen: something important, really important. Mathew felt confident that this would not be just a casual introduction. He had heard so much about this distinguished man from Page that he felt he knew Morse intimately. And everything he knew about him he liked. To himself Mathew repeated a dozen times a day, "O, I do hope he likes me. It would be a most fortunate thing."

The golden wand of the Goddess of Fortune was now pointing definitely to New York City. From the mountain farm it had pointed to Saratoga Springs and had led Mathew to the studio of William Page, then to Albany. Now it moved on.

One more giant step and Brady would be in a great

metropolis. Then he would be close to that glorious horizon of history that was destined to envelop him so completely and make him rich, famous, and beloved! The wand of Fortune pointed the way, but the Goddess herself was silent. What she knew she did not disclose; she did not even whisper it in a dream. For at that very moment, in far-off France, there was, besides Morse, another artist working on an invention, one completely different from the telegraph, but just as revolutionary.

Fate had brought together the American and the French artists. They had much in common. Both were painters. Both had a love of mechanics and science. Both had curiosity and originality. They understood each other. And at once they became friends. The American Morse was to have the great honor and distinction of bringing the discovery of his French friend to America. The name of the French artist would become famous overnight. His name was Louis Jacques Mandé Daguerre.

It was his invention that would take hold of the young Mathew Brady and bring him, in a final giant leap, on to the stage of American history. And this would be his final step to fame and fortune.

One morning Mathew arrived at Page's studio to find the artist entirely absorbed in a letter that had just arrived from Paris.

"It's from Morse," Page said without looking up. "Come here and sit down. I want to read you. . . . I do not quite make it out. It is all most curious. There is a secret discovery and yet the secret will soon be disclosed. It will all be made public because it is so tremendous that the French government. . . . Let me see what Morse says about this."

Page went back over the letter. "Yes, here it is. It is so important that the French government is buying the invention and will grant the inventor a yearly pension of 6,000 francs for the rest of his life."

"But what is it?" asked young Brady.

"Ah! He has been sworn to secrecy. He is a little vague about it. He says it is one of the most beautiful discoveries of the age. It is not electrical but rather chemical and partly physical. It is done on a small sheet of copper that becomes like a silver mirror. That is not the important part of the discovery. The important thing is that the mirror has a memory and can retain something that has been reflected upon it."

He paused to think before he again looked at the letter and added, "Morse says that artists would find this most valuable in their work, for it would greatly reduce the number of sittings necessary to complete a portrait."

"A mirror with a memory," repeated young Brady. This was indeed strange. "How can a mirror have a memory?"

"It sounds most fantastic and even unbelievable and yet . . ." Page hesitated, holding the letter in his hand, weighing it. "Had it come from someone else I could easily dismiss it as something imagined and exaggerated. But my dear friend Morse is not easily taken in. He is practical, he has good hands, he could build a clock and each wheel would cog into the next. That is how his mind works: logical, reasonable, exact. He would not write all this with such enthusiasm unless. . . . I know him and when he says it is one of the most wonderful discoveries of our age then. . . . Certainly it must be."

Young Brady was filled with wonder. His lips whispered, "A mirror with a memory. . . . Copper plate covered with silver and on the silver an image. . . . A mirror with a memory."

Morse also wrote a letter to a newspaper, the New York *Observer,* in which he gave a brief account of the Daguerre process. This letter appeared several weeks after Page had received his letter. Evidently the process was now no longer held in secrecy. This newspaper account only renewed the curiosity burning in Page and young Brady.

They could not stop talking and wondering. There was an excitement in the air, something impending. Summer was drawing to a close. The days were growing shorter. A coolness in the air announced the coming autumn. Page seemed restless and a little depressed.

One morning when young Brady came into the studio, Page looked up from his work and said, "Mathew, do you remember a promise I once made you?"

"I certainly do."

"What was it?" Page knew what it was but he wanted to see if Mathew did remember.

"We would take a trip to New York together. And you would introduce me to your friend Samuel Morse."

"Yes, that is right. I promised. And what I promised. . . . Yes, I did say we would take a trip and when I said it. . . . The summer is almost over. As you know there is not much work to be had in Albany in the wintertime. I tried it here some years ago—almost no commissions at all."

"Perhaps there are other places that do not close down so completely," said Brady.

"That is just what I have been thinking. In fact my friends have often proposed that I consider a move, and even Morse has suggested it."

"Where to?"

"To New York, of course. In New York there is always life and activity. Summer or winter, rain or snow, it makes no difference. And here in Albany. . . . That is what I have been thinking about. And so when I said that perhaps we would take a trip. . . . This will be more than a trip, for we will not be coming back."

"The studio equipment could go down by river boat," young Mathew suggested. "I could get hold of some large crates. So when you decide, then I can start packing. I have it all organized in my mind."

"Mathew, you would like New York."

"I'm sure I would. So when you decide—"

"I've already decided. Let's go as soon as we can. We could probably be there even before Morse arrives. He is coming on the *British Queen,* due to leave Portsmouth on the third of September. While the *British Queen* is the fastest ship on the Atlantic, the weather in September does not always make for a good crossing. But it doesn't matter who reaches New York first. It will be good to see Morse. You can start packing at once."

While Page was talking, young Mathew had gone to the end of the studio and was rummaging among an odd assortment of picture frames.

"I have already begun," he announced.

Chapter **2**

Photography Is Born

The *British Queen,* with Samuel Morse aboard, docked at New York on September 20, 1839. That year marked a great turning point in the life of Mathew Brady. From this time on he was to be involved with men and women and events of American history. In the end, just as the Goddess of Fortune had whispered, he was to cover a vast panorama of history, a stretch of time reaching backward to the founding fathers of the Republic and forward into the 20th century.

It all began with Samuel Morse, who brought back from France with him a fully detailed description of the Daguerre process, as well as a daguerreotype camera that he had made for him in Paris. It was an exact copy of the one used by his friend Daguerre. This was the magic box that was capable of capturing an image.

Morse's studio was exactly as Page had described it to young Mathew, a jumble of confusion, a tangle of wires, jars of batteries, coils, magnets, boxes, and bags of chemicals. Now, added to the jumble on the table beside a model of his telegraph stood the camera made for him in France.

Morse received William Page and his young protégé Mathew Brady with open arms. The older man cleared some chairs and made the two of them comfortable. To catch up with all the news, Morse asked many questions and was glad to learn that his former pupil, Page, had finally come to settle in New York City. While Page was answering his questions, Morse, with the trained eye of the portrait painter and his generous heart, glanced now and again at young Brady. Occasionally Morse managed to get the youth into the conversation.

Morse saw before him a genial youth, slim, gentle, frail, and soft spoken. Young Brady's features were delicate except for his nose, which was fairly pronounced. His hands were small and his fingers narrow. His blue eyes were deeply set. At times they seemed serious and reflected the absorbed state of his mind. But at other times they had in them a lively twinkle. His glance was frank and friendly. His smile was winning. He was a bit shy, but in reply to some of Morse's questions, he spoke rapidly, almost bubbling over with youthful enthusiasm. He was excited about many things: painting, nature, animals, his

[22]

trip down from Albany, and the dazzling wonder of New York City. His soft speech had that happy Irish quality of outgoing warmth.

In short, everything that Morse observed about Mathew was likable. This attractiveness was a natural asset that would make him many, many friends in all stations of life, high and low. Page had been the first. And now Morse too was becoming a good friend.

Morse could see his visitors' eyes were riveted on the camera he had brought from Paris. "Here," he said, "let me show you something." He drew out of a case a small copper plate. On its silvered surface, they could see, sharply defined, a street scene.

"It's the Unitarian Church!" explained Page.

"I took it only yesterday from the stairway window on the third story of the University. I was showing John Draper, our chemistry professor, how it was done. He has been experimenting on his own, and now he is building a camera like mine for himself."

The visitors gazed a long time at the image of the Unitarian Church on the silvered surface of the copper plate. It was curious, new and completely different from anything they had ever seen or imagined. There was something about the picture that captured the imagination and held it prisoner. The shiny metal plate was truly a mirror with a memory. Over and over again they examined it, hardly realizing that this was perhaps the very first picture ever taken in America. Only the Goddess of Fortune could at that moment have known that very soon this picture would be followed by millions upon millions of others.

Morse explained briefly that a sheet of copper plated with silver was first washed in nitric acid and then buffed to a high polish. Then in the dark, the silvered plate was exposed in a small box to iodine vapors until the surface of the plate turned a deep golden yellow. This coating took only a short time, a half minute or less. The iodine made the silvered surface sensitive to light. The plate was then put in the camera while the room was still dark, and then the cap was taken off the lens of the camera and the plate exposed to the light. The time required for an image to form on the plate varied from a few minutes to over an hour, depending on the strength of the sunlight. Finally, the image was brought out by heating mercury so that its vapor covered the exposed plate. Finally the plate was plunged in a bath of hyposulfite to fix the image permanently.

"It all sounds most complicated," Morse concluded. "But when you see it done—and I will soon show you—then it is not too involved. My friend Daguerre has just written a book describing the whole process in detail. I am expecting a copy by the next mail boat."

"Did this idea come suddenly to your friend Daguerre?" asked Page.

"Not at all. He has been working on this process for more than ten years. First with his partner, Nicéphore Niepce, for it was Niepce who had some of the original ideas. Niepce's son, Isidore, is getting 4,000 francs a year

[24]

for them from the French government, just as Daguerre is getting 6,000 francs a year. Niepce died about six years ago, and since then Daguerre has worked alone and made the process practical. As you know, the French government has taken over this discovery and has made it public at a joint meeting of the Academy of Sciences and the Academy of Fine Arts. That took place last August 19th. The excitement in Paris, in fact in all Europe, knew no bounds."

During the next few weeks Morse demonstrated the daguerreotype process to many of his friends, including Page and Brady. One bright sunny day Morse took a picture of his wife and daughter as they sat on the roof of the University building. The sun was very bright; and since the exposure was between ten and twenty minutes, his sitters kept their eyes closed. But he had a good picture, perhaps the first portrait study taken in the United States. Professor Draper of the Chemistry Department in the University also made a portrait photograph of his sister about the same time, and so it is not certain which was the very first.

Soon many clever people all over America were experimenting with photography. The process had been clearly described in Europe, and many U.S. newspapers had carried the account of it. The New York *Herald* called it "The New Art," and told how the camera must be held rigid "for eight or ten minutes, directed to the object to be represented." Then it added with pride, "In

Europe a longer exposure is required, because an American sun shines brighter than the European." The newspaper described the final result: "It looks like fairy work, and changes its colors like a chameleon . . . . It is the first time that the rays of the sun were ever caught on this continent and imprisoned, in all their glory."

Photography was a kind of fever that infected many people in many places.

The 79 page pamphlet that Daguerre prepared, as part of his contract with the French government, was now in print. His instructions were so complete that they could be followed by anyone who had a grain of scientific intelligence. The camera was clearly described and could be built by any good instrument maker. So great was the interest and excitement that within five months the pamphlet went through more than 30 different editions. It was translated into English, Spanish, German, Swedish, and even Russian.

There was something novel and romantic about this process. What it produced seemed magical. And many men with time on their hands began building cameras so that they could become master magicians.

In the United States, before the year was out, photographers were active in New York, Boston, Philadelphia, and many other cities. Even during this first year important progress was made in two directions. A double lens was now mounted in a brass barrel which allowed 16 times more light to enter the camera than did the single lens used by Daguerre. At the same time the sensitivity of the plate was increased by the addition of bromine. These two improvements at once made photography more practical. For now it was possible to take portraits with exposures of less than a minute.

Hundreds of people were eager to have their pictures taken. And there were many men who were eager to become photographers if only they could learn the technique of this involved process.

Who could teach photography? Morse, of course. And he did.

Having given up painting to develop his invention of the telegraph and having spent a good deal on his trip to France, Morse found himself with little money. His position at the University paid very poorly. But so many people besieged him to teach them the new process that he decided to give a course in photography so that he could continue to work on perfecting his telegraph instrument.

For a full course of instruction in the preparation of the plates and the taking and developing of daguerreotypes Morse charged $25. This was America's first school of photography.

Some of his pupils became well known as pioneers of American photography. Samuel Broadbent of Philadelphia and Albert S. Southworth of Boston distinguished themselves in portraiture. Edward Anthony, an engineer, later organized the first company to manufacture supplies for photographers. Still more important, was a

[27]

young fellow named Mathew Brady who had come from a mountain farm.

The Goddess of Fortune had finally brought young Brady together with photography. From the very first they seemed made for each other. Destiny was ready to take over. From then on Brady and photography were to be together until his very last day.

Chapter **3**

Brady's Little Old New York

Sixteen-year-old Mathew now had two great excitements in his life, photography and New York City. Here was a busy, rapidly growing metropolis pulsing with life. For Mathew every street had something curious, strange, and fascinating.

Soon after arriving from Albany, William Page opened a studio on Chambers Street. For a time Mathew lived with him and earned his keep by serving the painter as a kind of Man Friday, as he had done in Albany. But then Brady found a job in Alexander T. Stewart's dry-goods store. Stewart had come to the United States from Ireland about 20 years before and become one of New York's pioneer merchants. He found Brady friendly and attractive, and not only gave him a job but encouraged him to improve himself in his spare time.

Mathew enrolled in Morse's photography course, and he also continued to help Page in his studio. Mathew soon discovered that his casemaking skill was much in demand, for the city had a growing trade of jewelers and surgical and scientific instrument makers. Cases were also needed for framing the artists' miniature portraits that were so popular. Now that a number of photographers were establishing studios to take daguerreotypes, more and more cases were needed. To keep the delicate silver surface from tarnishing, it was necessary to put a piece of glass over the finished daguerreotype and to seal the edges with tape so that air could not get in. A little case hid the taped edges and framed the picture. Morse himself was adding to his meager income by taking pictures. It is very probable that Brady paid for his photography lessons with cases for Morse's daguerreotypes.

Mathew was still quite small and slight in build; indeed, he always remained so, but he was wiry and full of energy. He worked in Stewart's store, studied photography with Morse, built himself a camera, and even conducted experiments on his own. All these things he was able to do and still have time left for casemaking.

He had time also to join in the life of the great city. There was so much to see and so much to learn. The city was a new kind of school for him, a school of life and experience. And young Mathew was an impressionable and eager student.

In those years many young boys came to New York; and if they had energy, prudence, and industry, they made their marks. Social barriers were swept aside. Democracy played no favorites. Every youth had a chance. In almost every street of old New York, Brady saw the marks of success and heard encouraging tales of those who had risen from poverty to wealth.

For instance, a Yankee boy, David Reynolds had arrived some years before at the age of 14, hungry, weary after a long journey, and without a penny in his pocket. At the Bowery, close to City Hall, he leaned against a tree to rest. A well dressed gentleman approached Reynolds and asked him if he would carry his trunk to the wharf. Reynolds was glad to do it, and the gentleman gave him 25 cents. With this money, Reynolds bought some fruit at the wharf and returned to the friendly tree. He ate some of the fruit and sold the rest. Thus he began.

He continued to sell fruit under the tree. Soon he had a thriving fruit stand, then a shop, then he bought two adjacent buildings, and finally he pulled them all down and built the North American Hotel. By the time young Mathew arrived in New York, the hotel was a lively place, advertising that its table was "constantly furnished with every luxury of a plentiful New York market." The tree had had to be cut down to make room for the hotel, but David Reynolds loved the tree so much that he had a sculptor carve his statue out of the trunk. In this way, he expressed his gratitude for the fortune that had grown from his fruit stand sheltered in the shade of tree's branches.

There were a hundred stories like David Reynolds'. Enterprise was on the march. Everywhere there was bustle and lively activity.

The wharves of lower Manhattan were uniquely active. There Mathew saw great sailing vessels arrive almost daily from distant shores with strange cargoes and odd looking foreign crews. New York had surpassed Boston and Philadelphia in shipping and was now the busiest port in the United States. Just a year before Brady reached New York, fast Atlantic steam packets—long, slim sidewheelers—began regular transatlantic service.

It was all most exciting. Not far from Page's studio on Chambers Street, young Mathew saw the place where George Washington had been inaugurated as the first President of the United States. On those very paving stones had walked John Adams, Thomas Jefferson, Alexander Hamilton, Robert Livingston, James Madison, and that whole distinguished group of American statesmen who attended the birth of the new government.

Young Mathew walked indeed on historic ground. There he touched a past that marked the beginnings of a land growing so rapidly that it almost staggered the imagination. When the government had moved from New York to Philadelphia in 1790, everything it possessed, the furniture and books of Congress, the Supreme Court, and the President's office, was transported in three horse-drawn wagons. Now the United States stretched west to the Pacific and had on the Mississippi River alone more shipping tonnage than all of the British Isles. In 1790 when the first census was taken, the population of the United States had been less than 4,000,000. By the time Brady was born in 1823, it had jumped to 10,000,000. When young Mathew came to New York, it stood at 17,-000,000. When Brady went to Washington just before the Civil War, the people of the land numbered 31,000,000. And before Brady closed his eyes for the last time near the end of the century, the population stood at 70,000,-000.

America was on the march. Wherever young Mathew looked, he could see phenomenal growth. Life was pulsing. New York was exciting. Every day shiploads of immigrants arrived. All the languages of the world could be heard on the streets of New York.

The rapidly growing population gave birth to a new kind of journalism. In 1833 the New York *Sun* had been founded, and two years later James Gordon Bennett had started his *Herald*. About a year after Brady's arrival, Horace Greeley's *Tribune* was launched. Among these newspapers there was a keen rivalry. Each tried to outdo the others in gathering the news and presenting it in a lively manner.

In New York, young Brady found a rich cultural life, too—colleges, professional schools, libraries, museums, and flourishing theatres. There were other popular entertainments: a bearbaiting pit; a pit where pedigreed terriers could demonstrate their rat-killing skill; and

[*33*]

prize fight rings. A private menagerie, elegantly named the Zoological Institute, was not far from David Reynolds' North American Hotel. In 1839, P. T. Barnum was writing advertisements for this zoo. In 1841, he bought the American Museum at Broadway and Ann Street, and began his sensational career in earnest. He and Brady were destined to become good friends. From Barnum, Brady learned the value of publicity. To the names of Page and Morse must be added that of Barnum as contributors to Mathew Brady's early success. Barnum persuaded many notables to pose before Brady's camera.

So much that was new and different did Brady see in New York: gas-lighted streets; shop windows illuminated at night; street vendors with their distinctive calls; well dressed women in carriages; poor women—wives of hawkers and tradesmen—walking in the streets; newsboys on the run; men on horseback racing up Broadway. In the morning, boys were running to school; in the evening, many a laborer staggered home under the load of too much drink; at night the fashionable world filled the restaurants and theatres; the less fashionable sang ballads in the many saloons. New York City was a river of life as rushing as any mountain stream. Nothing held it back in its onward surge. All this was the New York of Brady's youth.

But there was another side to life in New York, a sordid side. With overcrowding, bad sanitary conditions, and extremes of wealth and poverty, the loafer emerged as a bold gangster. Gangs often grew out of hand. The police tried hard to hold them in check, but from time to time riots broke out. Added to this human affliction, periodic epidemics of yellow fever, smallpox, and cholera swept the city. The streets were filthy, and the manure of many horses was pounded down to a solid crust that covered the roadways. Rain created ugly puddles. New York was a city of contrasts. There was the silk and lace of high society and the crude brown burlap of poverty and crime.

A good part of the business section of the city, destroyed by fire in 1834, had still not been rebuilt. A serious panic in 1837 had created a shortage of money, and money was still hard to come by in 1840. Many men were out of work. Recovery came very slowly. The depression had spread over the entire land. Because of the hard times, many men who had little or no employment responded eagerly to the startling discovery of photography. Many thought that here was a new venture they might turn to profit. Everybody, it seemed, wanted his picture taken. Customers were many and at first few could meet the demand. So, in a very short time, there was a mushroom growth of daguerreotype galleries. It was a new and rushing business. But only a few men had a talent and feeling for this new art, photography.

Such was New York shortly after young Brady came there. In this social and economic environment, his character was formed.

Chapter 4

Brady's Broadway Gallery

After five years in bustling New York, Brady, then 21, felt his apprenticeship had come to an end. He knew what he wanted to do. The year was 1844.

During these five years he had learned as much from Morse as he could, and he had made friends with a good many of Morse's pupils. Some of these men had become professional photographers. Edward Anthony, who was to join with Brady in a business venture in the 1850's, had been trained as a civil engineer, and after studying with Morse, he took his daguerreotype camera up to the Canadian border. His pictures there reportedly helped the United States settle a boundary dispute with Great Britain in 1842. The pictures supposedly showed that some highlands England claimed did not in reality exist. If such use was made of Anthony's pictures, this was the first practical use of photography by any government.

Other pupils of Morse stayed on in New York or went back to their hometowns and opened galleries to feed the public's sudden appetite for having their pictures taken. But young Mathew Brady was not in a hurry. He needed capital, and so he continued working at Stewart's, saving every penny that he could.

At the same time he experimented on his own and became quite proficient with his homemade camera. He also continued his casemaking, supplying a number of jewelers as well as Morse's pupils, who had become professional photographers. Being an accepted member of the first group of American photographers proved a decided advantage to young Brady. He was in constant touch with all the new technical developments. He exchanged information on the basis of professional equality. His casemaking brought him into almost daily contact with these photographers.

His apprenticeship was over. He knew exactly what he wanted. On the busiest corner in downtown New York, Broadway and Fulton Street, he rented the top floor of a three-story wooden building. Since he had been in the casemaking business, he probably knew the jeweler who occupied the store on the first floor. Barnum's Museum was diagonally across the street.

From Morse's experiments, Brady knew that better light produced better pictures. So he hired carpenters to rip up sections of the roof and install glass skylights. These worked so well that they were at once copied by other photographers. But Brady had other innovations. He designed reflectors to better control the direction and quality of the light and to shorten the time of exposure of the plate. In those days, exposures ranged from four to forty seconds.

Many people could not sit still for so long a time, and so to help the sitter hold his head quiet, photographers devised a contraption called an "immobilizer." This consisted of an iron rod set into a heavy stand, with two small adjustable pads that fitted into the back of the sitter's head, thus holding it steady. The "immobilizer" saved many a plate that would otherwise have been ruined. Since the contraption was behind the sitter, it did not, of course, show in the picture.

Soon Brady's dark rooms and "operating room," as the room where pictures were taken was called, were ready. He had two cameras and two "immobilizers." The gallery also had a dressing room where patrons could arrange themselves for their sittings. Brady hired painters to letter boldly across the entire front of the building above his windows: Brady's Daguerrian Miniature Gallery. He had learned, probably from his showman friend P. T. Barnum, that it was a mistake to hide your light under a bushel.

The huge sign proved to be just the right thing. For no sooner were the doors opened than there was an onrush of business. From the very first day, Brady enjoyed prosperity and paid little attention to his rivals and powerful competitors.

Success was just over the horizon. Brady played his part. He ordered clothes in the best fashion and taste to be made by a good tailor. He moved to the fashionable Astor House, then located on Broadway close to his gallery. He felt that personal relations with people of society and distinction would be good for business. They were. All society flocked to his gallery, climbed the three flights of stairs, and, after making themselves as presentable as possible in the dressing room, came before Brady's camera.

He took his watch from his pocket, removed the lens cap, counted off the seconds. The picture had been taken.

While Brady had a number of assistants to help prepare his plates, develop them, and even to serve as cameramen for the portraits of his less distinguished visitors, still he superintended every detail of the process. He worked hard. He was up early, and often worked developing plates late at night when everyone else had left the gallery.

He had a keen sense of composition, disposing his subjects to the best advantages before the camera, and he was most careful with all the technical details of the process. The very year he opened his Broadway gallery, Brady, as a result of his endless striving for perfection, was awarded the first prize medal for the finest daguerreotype shown when the American Institute held its first photographic exhibition. Still he kept trying to make his daguerreotypes better and better. They continued to win the first prize for him at the American Institute exhibitions for the next four years. Prizewinning became a habit.

Prizes were good for business. They brought in customers. Brady was pleased to prove the artistic worth of his product in open competition, but still there was something he valued more than prizes. Good work was important, and good work accomplished with artistic taste made Brady's pictures a little better than those of his competitors. Yet even this superiority did not satisfy him.

Brady was conscious of the times in which he was living. He could see many of the spectacular changes that were being brought about by the rapid growth of America. Now that he had at his command the silver mirror with a memory, perhaps that mirror could record the people and passing events on this historical stage. To himself he said, "In the past, time rubbed out everything. But now the things that can be caught in the mirror will endure. Future generations will then be able to see this record on the mirror." Then he asked himself, "What would be worth recording? What would be the most significant and of the greatest value to future generations?"

These were the thoughts that occupied Brady's mind during that first year, a most successful year, after the opening of his Broadway gallery.

Brady's success was not unusual. He came in on the crest of a wave. Almost every daguerreotype gallery that opened in any city of the United States went well at the start.

In 1850, a few years after Brady opened his Broadway studio, there were in New York City alone 77 galleries employing 127 operators. Most of them were engaged in the business of making "likenesses." One gallery even advertised: "Families waited upon, in or out of the city, to take likenesses of sick or deceased persons, at moderate prices."

Beaumont Newhall in his illuminating *History of Photography from 1839 to the Present* tells how "Yankee ingenuity brought mechanical improvements. The tedious task of buffing the plates to a high polish was done by machinery." John Whipple installed a steam engine in his Boston gallery to run the buffing wheels, heat the mercury, fan the clients waiting their turn, and also "revolve a gilded sunburst on his sign outside the gallery." Another gallery, in Boston, had entertainment for clients as they waited in a well appointed lounge. Here were a piano, a music box, cages of singing birds, beautiful draperies, portraits on the walls, stained glass, statuary, everything designed "to impress the visitor . . . and serve to soothe the troubled spirit, and calm the anxious brow, preparatory to the obtaining of a good picture."

But not all pictures could possibly turn out good. The ugly lady who had never seen herself as she really looked had always imagined herself a beautiful princess. The daguerreotype did not improve her true image. She was shocked when she saw it and refused to pay for what she declared was a "monstrous distortion." She and many others like her quickly spread the word that photography was a failure. And the ugly ladies found many to agree with them: squint-eyed men, those with tics and twitches, and old people who could not keep their heads from nodding. But though these detractors cried loudly, their voices did not stop the onrush of business. Photography was a sensation.

The demand for daguerreotypes became so great that even the many galleries could not keep up with it. At the same time a price war broke out among the galleries serving the masses with a cheap product. The standard price of $1 per portrait dropped to 50 cents and then to 25 cents. With a double lens attached to the camera, portraits were taken "two at a pop" for 12½ cents each.

Newhall records that the work was speeded up in these "picture factories" by division of labor until some galleries were able to turn out 500 and even 1,000 daguerreotypes daily. "The sitter bought a ticket and was posed by an operator who never left the camera. A plate, already prepared by the polisher and the coater, was brought to him, and he passed it on exposed, in its protective shield, to the mercuralizer who developed it, to the gilder who enriched it, and to the artist who tinted it: fifteen minutes later the customer exchanged his ticket for the finished likeness." This kind of slapdash, mass production was not satisfactory. Many customers were disappointed.

Brady saw what was happening all about him, but he was never tempted to turn his gallery into a factory. He was well satisfied with his business and refused to cheapen his product. In the face of heavy competition he maintained his prices and also the quality of his workmanship. He tried constantly to attract a clientele who would appreciate a superior product.

Every now and then from the very beginning, even during the first year in his Broadway gallery, Brady was haunted by this question: How could he capture the thing that was significant, the thing that was important and would remain important for future generations? This problem possessed him. As he kept turning it in his mind the question itself seemed to take on a silver polish. It glistened and glowed with an inner light. At last he had it.

It was all so natural, for it was all part of the same thing. It was as though the vision of the golden wand of the Goddess of Fortune had returned once more to point out the way.

History again loomed on the horizon. And now the horizon was closer. It seemed almost at hand. The whole panorama of history was spread out before him. He felt it so close to him that one more step would take him into the midst of it, and he would become part of it.

From now on history would be his life and his destiny.

Chapter 5

History Sits for Its Portrait

Brady's plan was simple. He decided to use his camera to record for posterity pictures of his most distinguished contemporaries. From these daguerreotypes he would have large lithographs made. For each picture he would have a suitable text written by a distinguished writer. Then when all was complete, Brady planned to publish the portraits in a large volume entitled *The Gallery of Illustrious Americans.*

A few illustrious Americans he knew would in time come to his gallery. But he also knew that Fame is fickle and shy. And Fame is often modest and does not come forward boldly. Also Fame would not climb three flights of stairs to his gallery without a little persuasion or inducement.

[45]

Such friends as P. T. Barnum, who owned the museum across the street and knew almost everybody in New York, helped him. Barnum was a fine salesman and easily persuaded many important people to be photographed by Brady. He hoped others might come and thus build his reputation so that he could specialize in the portraiture of illustrious Americans. He decided that he would make enlarged copies of any pictures he took of very distinguished people. These portraits he would mount on the walls of his gallery lounge. This public display would give him prestige. In time, Brady was sure that his walls would be covered with pictures of America's most famous people. This display would in turn attract others. And in time Fame would willingly climb the three flights to his gallery.

Ironically enough, Brady's earliest portrait of an illustrious American may not have been taken by him at all. About a year after Brady opened his Broadway gallery, he learned that Andrew Jackson, who had served as seventh President of the United States, lay quite ill at his home, the Hermitage, near Nashville, Tennessee. When "Old Hickory," as his friends affectionately called him, had come to the capital for his inauguration, he had brought with him a whole rough-hewn, tobacco-chewing crew of western patriots. But that had been years before. Even earlier, how many battles Jackson had fought and won for his country! How many duels he had fought for his honor! What a stormy life, filled with hatreds, intrigue, and romance. Now Brady knew that Jackson was near his end. Here was history, now breathing its last. If he wanted to capture a rare, fleeting glimpse of it, he would have to act quickly.

It is not certain today whether Brady packed up his equipment and journeyed himself to the Hermitage, or whether he had the picture that ultimately hung on his gallery wall taken by a Nashville photographer, Dan Adams. Years later, in an interview, Brady said he "sent to the Hermitage" and had the picture taken. Marquis James, the leading biographer of Jackson in the 20th century, says Brady himself took the picture on April 15, 1845. To add to the confusion, Anthony, Edwards, and Company claimed to have taken the picture.

Whoever took the picture, the result is magnificent. The dying old man could not hide his illness from the camera, but his courage and spirit and the fire of his eyes were recorded for all time. It is the only photograph of Jackson in existence and the finest portrait of him. He died less than two months after the picture was taken.

In time Brady photographed all the Presidents of the United States from John Quincy Adams, the sixth President, to and including William McKinley, the twenty-fourth, with but one exception: William Henry Harrison, who died in 1841 before Brady started his career. Altogether, Brady managed to photograph 19 Presidents!

He did not photograph all of these Presidents while they were in the White House. Some, such as John Quincy Adams, he photographed after their terms of office had

[47]

expired. Some he photographed, as we will soon see, even before they were elected to the Presidency.

One day Brady noticed that Edgar Allan Poe, the poet and short story writer, had come into his gallery. He had not come to have his picture taken, however, but was merely accompanying his poet-friend William Ross Wallace, who had an appointment for a sitting.

Brady could see that Poe was in a melancholy mood. Poverty and the illness of his wife had reduced him to a sorry state. Nevertheless, Brady was eager to take Poe's picture. When the photographer had finished with Wallace, he turned to Poe and asked him if he would care to sit for his portrait. But Poe quickly shook his head. Brady guessed the reason for this quick refusal. He really had not made himself clear, for he could see that the poet thought this was going to cost him something. Brady quickly apologized and explained that he had not intended to make any charge for the picture. He was an admirer of Poe's writing, and so would be honored to have his picture to hang in the lounge. And, of course, he would give him some copies free.

At length, with Wallace's help, Poe was persuaded, and Brady could uncap his lens. The result was a most startling and beautiful portrait of one of America's greatest literary figures.

Brady was not always successful in persuading distinguished Americans to sit before his camera. He once went to Boston to see if he could photograph some of the famous literary people there. In fact, Henry Wadsworth

Longfellow, the famous poet, had promised to sit for him. ·
But alas, Longfellow never showed up for his appointment. And Brady returned to New York without any pictures. Still, he was not bitter about it, or resentful. Brady
ignored his occasional failures, for he knew that in time
he would have many illustrious Americans. He would
manage without the Boston literary notables. And he did.

Inspired by his idea of publishing a large handsome
volume, *The Gallery of Illustrious Americans,* Brady in
1847 got up courage to write President Polk in Washington, where Brady had set up a temporary gallery to photograph politicians when Congress was in session. The President, whose term of office would soon end, replied with
great courtesy, inviting Brady to bring his camera to the
White House. At the appointed time Brady arrived with
his equipment and his assistant. The sitting was evidently quite painless, for Polk, in his diary, recorded it all very
casually, "I yielded to the request of an artist named
Brady of New York by sitting for my Daguerreotype likeness today. I sat in the large dining room."

While in Washington, Brady looked about. He found
that a number of galleries already were in operation
there, some having been well established for a good while.
Competition in Washington would be quite serious, yet
Brady felt that here was the place where most illustrious Americans were to be found. In Washington, history was made. And it was the men of history that
he desired to record.

Brady was confident that a permanent gallery in Washington, in spite of the competition, would attract many of the important people in the government. Certain people had promised to help him. So he decided to maintain his most profitable gallery in New York and open a second permanent one in Washington.

In New York Brady added two distinguished literary men to his portrait gallery: James Fenimore Cooper, author of the popular *Leatherstocking Tales,* and Washington Irving, author of *Rip Van Winkle* and *The Legend of Sleepy Hollow.* His collection was growing.

Brady once confessed that he was never overbold or aggressive, and that his quiet and gentle nature was perhaps an advantage. "Certainly," he said, "it helped me out with genuine men." Then he went on to relate how it happened that Cooper became camera shy. He was sitting one day for his daguerreotype at another New York gallery when the photographer, just to make conversation, most tactlessly brought up a recent quarrel reported in the newspapers between Cooper and his publisher. Cooper jumped up from his chair and stormed out of the gallery. After that he refused to allow any one to take his picture.

But Brady plucked up his courage and ventured to Cooper's hotel. "He came out in his morning gown," said Brady, "and asked me to excuse him until he had dismissed a caller. I told him what I had come for." There was a pause. Cooper looked at Brady. He saw him as everyone saw him, gentle and friendly. "Cooper said, 'How far is it to your gallery?' 'Only two blocks.' "

So it was that Brady won Cooper over. In a little while they were walking down Broadway together. "He stayed for two hours," said Brady, "had half a dozen sittings."

To Brady's literary men were added the pictures of two well-known stage celebrities: Jenny Lind, the singer who was known as The Swedish Nightingale, and the famous Austrian dancer, Fanny Elssler.

While Jenny Lind had come to America in 1850 under the management of Brady's friend P. T. Barnum, it was not Barnum who was able to persuade the popular opera singer to visit Brady's gallery and pose for her picture. Since every gallery in New York was trying to get her picture, Barnum felt he could play no favorites. But it happened that Brady had a Swedish friend who in his youth had gone to school with Jenny. This man was kind enough to write the singer, who lost no time in visiting Brady's gallery. Seeing her carriage in the street, many people waited to catch sight of her. So great was the crowd that the police had to be called.

Jenny Lind's sensational tour in America, mainly under Barnum's auspices, brought her $1,000 a performance, a fabulous sum for those days. In all, before she left the shores of America she had gathered in $750,000. For Brady, Jenny Lind's sittings were quite profitable, too, for he sold hundreds of copies of his charming portraits of her. He sold also hundreds of copies of his portrait of Fanny Elssler, who thought Brady's work quite remarkable and ordered a number of prints of distinguished Americans to take back with her to Europe.

Brady also succeeded in adding another famous President to his collection of illustrious Americans: John Quincy Adams, sixth President of the United States. When Adams was in the White House, his Vice-President had been the eminent Southern champion, John Calhoun. The brilliant orator, Henry Clay, apostle of compromise between the South and the North, served as Adams' secretary of state. Now Adams, an old man, was devoting all his energies to defending the antislavery cause in the House of Representatives. Brady was later to come to know and photograph both Calhoun and Clay. And Brady himself was to be very much involved in the antislavery cause. The Goddess of Fortune was making her moves to bring all the far-flung forces together.

Exactly how Brady managed to get John Quincy Adams to sit for his portrait is not known. But it certainly was an achievement; for Adams, like James Fenimore Cooper, was known to be camera shy. Adams had had a bad experience in an upstate New York town, where he had been persuaded to enter a daguerreotype parlor. He recorded in his diary that "Four likenesses were made. . .all hideous." Brady's picture of Adams is a very remarkable likeness and a very valuable daguerreotype, for this courageous champion of freedom died not long after the picture was taken.

Brady now recognized that history was not static. History was organic. It was ever passing before him. To capture it, he had to be aware of its presence and of its movement. And he had to be bold enough to act.

Chapter 6

Washington and Romance

Brady was in his middle twenties when he opened his first gallery in Washington in 1847. He found a suitable loft over a jewelry store centrally located on Pennsylvania Avenue, which linked the White House with the Capitol. Either with forethought or by intuition, he dropped the name daguerreotype and called his Washington place the National Photographic Art Gallery. He trained his assistants so that he could go to New York as often as it was necessary. When in Washington, Brady always stayed at the National Hotel.

In Washington he had seven competitors, as well as competition from several popular photographers who visited the city from time to time. But he had anticipated this keen competition when he decided on the venture.

He knew that other photographers were after business. But he was after history as well. And this made a difference, an important difference between Brady and his rivals.

By good fortune, soon after Brady's arrival he was sponsored by two distinguished ladies in Washington society. The first was Mrs. Dolley Madison, wife of President Jefferson's secretary of state who later became the fourth President of the United States. Living in the Executive Mansion when it was set on fire by the British during the War of 1812, Dolley Madison had had the courage and good sense to save some of the government's treasures, including a full-length portrait of George Washington. At the time that Brady met Dolley Madison and took her picture, she was 80 years old. As a leader of Washington society and an admirer of Brady's portraits, she took great pains to introduce him to people who might be helpful.

The other distinguished lady who sponsored Brady in Washington was none other than Mrs. Alexander Hamilton, widow of the first U.S. secretary of the treasury, who had put the struggling young nation on such a solid financial footing. Mrs. Hamilton was 91 when Brady took her picture. One day some time later she brought him a small oval miniature painting of Hamilton and asked if Brady could make a faithful copy by the daguerreotype process. Brady could and was very happy to do so. Thus he added Alexander Hamilton to his portrait gallery. It is from this copy of a precious minature that the engraving of Hamilton used on United States $10 bills was made.

Everything went most smoothly for Brady despite keen competition. He found in Washington exactly what he had wanted. Not long after he had opened his Washington gallery, Brady was again invited to the White House. This time he photographed President Zachary Taylor and his entire Cabinet. From these pictures was made the first set of engravings of a President and his Cabinet ever published.

Then, soon afterward, Brady took the pictures of three of America's most brilliant statesmen: Daniel Webster, John Calhoun, and Henry Clay. He photographed them all during the winter of 1849-1850. Some of the sittings took place in the New York gallery and some in Washington.

In the very year that Brady took Webster's picture, the great orator used his eloquence to answer the Abolitionists in Congress and help preserve the Union. In his famous March 7th speech, he said, "I wish to speak today, not as a Massachusetts man, nor as a Northern man, but as an American. . . . I speak today for the preservation of the Union. 'Hear me for my cause.'" He spoke in favor of Clay's Compromise of 1850, which for a time removed the threat of slavery to the very existence of the Union. Not forever would the nation be able to avoid a conflict that would affect the life of every American, and that would make Mathew Brady even more famous.

Calhoun was just as distinguished as Webster, but he held very different political views. He had served as secretary of war under Monroe, had been twice elected Vice-President, and had also served as secretary of state. Calhoun's political philosophy furnished the South its main justification for secession from the Union.

Henry Clay, too, was a distinguished orator and statesman. As Democratic leader in Congress, he had been six times elected Speaker of the House. He had been John Quincy Adams' secretary of state. His compromises of the slavery question saved the Union three times. Brady photographed Clay in his New York gallery, making five different exposures. Then, in Washington, Clay came again to be photographed; and Brady took a few more exposures just to make sure he had something good. Calhoun came with his daughter to the Washington gallery. Webster visited the New York gallery, where Brady made five exposures.

The subsequent history of these three sets of daguerreotypes is extremely interesting. A few years after they were made and the wet-plate process had been invented, Brady copied the pictures and made good-sized enlargements of all three. These he hung on the walls of both his New York and Washington galleries. Then having photographed the enlargements on glass plates, he later made life-size enlargements on canvas and engaged two well-known artists to color these pictures and turn them into finished oil paintings.

Henry F. Darby painted the pictures of Clay and Calhoun, and Brady engaged John Neagle to paint the portrait of Webster. These three large paintings hung on the walls of his Washington gallery and were very much admired. At one time, after the Civil War, Brady was forced to mortgage the paintings. When he recovered financially, he retrieved them. Many years later, in 1881, the Joint Senate and House Committee on the Library, appointed to decorate the Capitol, bought the three pictures from Brady for $4,000. The Webster portrait brought $1,900 and the other two $2,100. They hang today in the main corridor of the Senate.

Soon after he had photographed these three great American statesmen, Brady was ready to publish the first part of his ambitious work, *The Gallery of Illustrious Americans*. He had intended to have John Howard Payne, the well-known actor, dramatist, and author of "Home Sweet Home," write the text to accompany each picture. But Payne had accepted an appointment to become the United States consul in Tunis and had to leave the country before he could even get started on Brady's project. So Brady engaged C. Edwards Lester, the foremost American art critic of his day, to write the text accompanying the pictures. Brady also engaged a well-known artist, Francis D'Avignon, to make the lithographs of each portrait, paying him $100 for each stone, a total of $1,200.

The *Gallery of Illustrious Americans* was a large volume, intended to be quite impressive on the parlor table. It sold for $30, a very high price for a single volume. A second volume was to follow with 12 more portraits. The illustrious men chosen for the first volume were: President Taylor; Calhoun; Webster; New York Senator and Governor Silas Wright; Clay; the explorer John Charles Frémont; John James Audubon, famous for his *Birds of America;* the historian William Hickling Prescott; General Winfield Scott; President Millard Fillmore; the Unitarian leader William Ellery Channing; and Lewis Cass, general and statesman. From this list, it can be seen that for Brady history was not limited solely to statesmen and generals.

The book, published in 1850, involved Brady in considerable expense. Reviews of the book were good, but the sales were poor. All in all, it was an artistic success but a financial failure. Though Brady continued working on a second volume, determined that history should be recorded, no more of *The Gallery of Illustrious Americans* appeared.

Brady's Washington gallery also had financial troubles. Competition in the capital was almost too much. Daguerreotypes were becoming cheap and very common. It has been estimated that early in the 1850's, 2,000 daguerreotypists were trying to make a living in the United States. Each year they produced something like 3,000,000 daguerreotypes! Some good portrait photographers willingly gave up their galleries to do other work. Eliphalet Brown, who made beautiful portraits, joined Commodore Matthew Perry in 1852 on his famous expedition that opened up Japan to the western world. Solomon N. Carvalho of Charleston was in 1853 chosen to join Fremont's western expedition and make daguerreotypes of the Rocky Mountains. In later years Brady was to copy many of Carvalho's beautiful western scenes by the wet-plate process. John M. Stanley used his camera on the expedition of Isaac Stevens in 1853 to find a route for the transcontinental railroad; the Indians were particularly delighted with his work.

One can get an idea of how low the daguerreotype had sunk in public opinion from the comment of one observer: "It was no uncommon thing to find watch repairers, dentists and other types of business folk to carry on daguerreotype on the side. I have known blacksmiths and cobblers to double up with it, as it was possible to have a horse shod, your boots tapped, a tooth pulled, or a likeness taken by the same man: verily, a man— a daguerreotype man—in his time, played many parts."

To add to the difficulties of this troublesome situation, Brady had difficulties with his Washington landlord, a Mr. Heydon, who wanted Brady to vacate the building. They even went to law over this, with the result that Brady was forced to abandon his Washington gallery. But he did not give up. He determined that he would someday return to Washington and reopen it. This promise he vowed he would carry out. And he did.

Before he left Washington, Brady had a wonderful experience. Later in life as an old man he spoke about this time and called it "the happiest moment" of his life.

According to one account Brady met the charming young lady who was later to become his wife at a dinner party given by a friend at the National Hotel in Washington—the hotel where Brady stayed when he came to Washington.

But Brady's biographer, James D. Horan, gives quite a different version of their first meeting. Horan got his information from Brady's two surviving relatives, his grandnieces Mrs. Mary H. Evans and Mrs. Alice H. Cox. These were the daughters of Brady's only nephew, Levin C. Handy, who became his heir.

According to Horan, Brady met the charming Julia Handy, not in Washington, but in nearby Maryland. Horan records that the setting for this romance was a "beautiful Maryland plantation—gay parties, hoopskirts, and young men who talked of nothing else but horses, duels, and manners of the time. It was all in the days that were swept away by the Civil War." It seems that Brady, according to the family legend, had been asked to come out to a picnic and dance given by a wealthy Maryland planter who had visited his Washington gallery to have his picture taken. Horan records that "There was little time for picnics and dances in the life of this dedicated and shy young man but something made Brady accept the invitation. And under the trees with the gay young people, Brady fell in love with the 'young miss' of the plantation, Julia Handy."

Her full name was Julia Elizabeth, but all her life long she was known to her friends as Julia. The daughter of a Maryland lawyer, Colonel Samuel Handy, she was related on her father's side to some of the oldest families who settled in Maryland long before the Revolution. On her mother's side she was related to a number of distinguished families in northern Virginia.

When Julia was four years old she had been taken on a visit to Washington and it was said that she was such a beautiful child that President Jackson was anxious to adopt her. But this is a legend which has little confirmation. Still, there is no doubt that Julia was a beautiful child, for the photographs which Brady made of this young lady just before and just after they were married show a serious face, serene, with clearly chiseled features, framed in a mass of dark curls.

They were married in the old E Street Baptist Church in Washington and went to live at the fashionable National Hotel. But they did not live there very long. When Brady closed his Washington gallery, they went to live in New York at the Astor House, situated almost directly opposite his New York gallery.

Theirs was a happy marriage for all the years of their lives. They lived quietly and avoided the gay society of New York and Washington. But they had many friends and Julia devoted herself to her husband and his work. Often she joined him in the evening when he was delayed in his gallery and kept him company during long hours in the laboratory and darkroom when work was pressing.

They had no children. Because of this they poured out their affection on their nephew Levin Handy, a child of Julia's brother. Brady later brought Levin Handy into his gallery and taught him everything he knew about photography. So it is that the legend of Brady's romance has come down to us through Levin Handy's two daughters, the grandnieces of Mathew Brady.

It is they, too, who recorded that in Brady's last years, as he sat in the parlor of his nephew's home, he recalled that the happiest moment of his entire life was that evening when he took Julia in his arms and danced to the strains of a melodious waltz. It was as though they were dancing on air floating away in a dream world of happiness.

FROM BRADY'S

The Gallery

of

Illustrious Americans

GENERAL
WINFIELD SCOTT

WILLIAM ELLERY
CHANNING

H. Clay

HENRY CLAY

JOHN JAMES
AUDUBON

WILLIAM HICKLING
PRESCOTT

JOHN CHARLES
FRÉMONT

PRESIDENT
MILLARD FILLMORE

D and Webster

DANIEL WEBSTER

GENERAL
ZACHARY TAYLOR

LEWIS CASS

J. C. Calhoun

JOHN CALDWELL CALHOUN

Chapter **7**

The Crystal Palace

Brady had been working very hard for a long time. His health had always been delicate, and unfortunately his eyes gave him trouble. Year by year the lenses of his eyeglasses got thicker. He was quite tired of doing the same thing over and over again. He had trained assistants to polish plates, to operate cameras, to develop the plates in the darkroom, and to take care of the myriad of details in the business. Then, too, he had made thousands of experiments, constantly seeking to improve his pictures. Now he was tired.

The business was prospering, and he badly needed a rest, a complete change. A trip to Europe could do it. Brady and his wife made up their minds.

[73]

In 1850 it was announced that the first great world's fair, the International Exhibition, would open officially in London in 1851, under the auspices of the Society of Arts and sponsored by its president, Prince Albert, husband of Queen Victoria. Much excitement arose when it was announced that a great hall, the Crystal Palace, was being constructed in Hyde Park to house the many exhibits. This iron and glass building, covering 20 acres, was built at a cost of almost $1,000,000. Excitement hit a fever pitch when it was announced that prizes were to be awarded for the best in art, science, invention, literature, and photography. Photographers of many lands were invited to send choice examples of their work.

In New York, many photographers ran through their files looking not only for good pictures but for novel ones, pictures that would catch the judges' eyes. Some photographers even advertised for unusual subjects in *Humphrey's Journal*, the first photographic magazine in the world. One photographer wanted a man or woman "over a hundred years old" to sit for a portrait. Another advertisement sought "a Revolutionary veteran to come forward to have his picture taken FREE." Since the Revolution had been fought some 70 years before, the veteran could hardly have been less than 90. Novelty seemed in the air, for many photographers felt that with hundreds of pictures coming to this competition from all over the world, only the novel, the strange, or the curious had any chance of attracting the attention of the judges.

Brady, however, did not agree with this reasoning. He needed no two-headed chickens or other freaks to gain the attention and respect of the jury. He got together a group of his very best portraits, 48 distinguished Americans, and sent them off to the Photographic Committee in London.

On May 1, 1851, the fair in the Crystal Palace was officially opened by Queen Victoria with her consort, Prince Albert, at her side. It had nearly 6,000 exhibits from England and about 500 from the English colonies; it also had more than 6,000 exhibits from foreign lands. All in all, the exhibitors numbered almost 14,000. Certainly this was the first great world's fair. It opened with a bang and was a tremendous success from the very first day.

Before the fair was over, more than 6,000,000 people had visited it. The great cost of the Crystal Palace was quickly repaid, and in the end there was a $1,000,-000 profit that the Society of Arts used to build the Victoria and Albert Museum.

Just two months after Queen Victoria opened the great fair, Mathew Brady and Julia sailed for England. Brady left his New York gallery in charge of a very able photographer, George S. Cook. Within about ten years, when the Civil War broke out, Brady would be photographer for the Union and Cook would be photographer for the Confederacy.

Sailing with the Bradys on the same ship were their friends, James Gordon Bennett, founder of the New York *Herald,* and his wife. It had been reported in the photographic journals that Mr. Brady would be gone from New York for a number of months. One editor wrote that while in Europe, Brady intended to visit Daguerre, the inventor of the process by which Brady had made so many fine pictures. Alas, Daguerre died while Brady was crossing the Atlantic.

Brady took his camera with him to Europe, as well as some of his best pictures. He hoped to photograph some of the famous people of the day there.

Photographers from the United States, Great Britain, France, Italy, Germany, and Austria had entered pictures at the fair. Altogether, 700 hung on the walls. But everyone admitted that the work done in the United States was superior.

All three medals awarded for daguerreotypes went to Americans. Martin M. Lawrence of Boston won a silver medal for an allegorical daguerreotype, "Past, Present, and Future," showing three girls facing left, forward, and right. John A. Whipple of Boston won a silver medal for a daguerreotype of the moon. The silver medal Brady received was for the general excellence of his 48 portraits. The catalog commented: "The brilliancy and sharpness of some of these are highly remarkable."

The *Illustrated London News* noted that the number of daguerreotype exhibiters was "very great, and the quality of production super-excellent. The likenesses of various distinguished Americans by Mr. Brady are noble examples of this style of art." Back in America, Horace Greeley, brilliant editor of the *Tribune,* wrote, "In daguerreotypes we beat the world."

Brady took a few pictures in Europe, but none of very great importance except, perhaps, that of Louis Napoleon, better known as Napoleon III, shortly after he had been proclaimed emperor of France. Brady had also written to the famous French writer, Victor Hugo, who promised to sit for his portrait; but it is not certain that he ever did so, for no picture of Hugo by Brady is known today.

Brady and Julia journeyed through France and Italy. This was a good time, a restful time. His health and strength were slowly restored. They visited the famous art museums of Florence and Rome and went down the Italian boot as far as Naples. Many places they went Brady was pleased to discover that his name and his work were quite well known.

Brady had two experiences in Europe that made definite contributions to his career. First, he saw an epoch-making photographic discovery demonstrated in London. Second, he met and became friends with a young Scot, Alexander Gardner.

English sculptor and photographer, Frederick Scott Archer. Two months before Queen Victoria opened the Crystal Palace, Archer announced his wet-plate process in *The Chemist.* With this process, photography took a giant step forward.

The wet-plate process had great advantages over the daguerreotype. To make a copy of a daguerreotype, it was necessary to rephotograph the original, but with the wet-plate process, the glass plate served as a negative from which any number of reprints could be made. Another advantage was that in the wet-plate process, prints were made on paper. It was also possible to make prints of great size. Thus full-sized portraits could be made. Still another advantage was that the glass plate could be retouched.

All this was most revolutionary. The daguerreotype had, as we have seen, become a cheap device in the hands of poorly skilled operators. The whole idea of photography was suffering from this cheapening. But now here was something entirely different.

Brady saw the new technique demonstrated in London. But he lacked knowledge of the chemistry involved. While he could see the possibilities of the new process, he hesitated to accept it. In time he did, and the wet-plate process was to help make Brady famous. It gave Brady, as well as photography, new life. At the same time it completely replaced and even destroyed the daguerreotype. Life and death came together, death for the daguerreotype and life for photography.

Alexander Gardner had come from Scotland. At 14 he had left school to take a job in a jeweler's shop. In the evenings he studied chemistry. When Gardner was

21 he had left the jeweler's shop and become a reporter for a Glasgow newspaper. His interest in chemistry brought him into photography. As an amateur, he made very fine daguerreotypes; and as soon as the Archer wet-plate process was made known, he was one of the first to try it and achieve successful results. Brady met Gardner, it is believed, in London during the fair. From the very first, they liked each other.

What Brady lacked, Gardner might easily supply. Brady recognized that Gardner's knowledge of chemistry as well as his ability with all technical processes would be of great advantage. And now with Brady's eyesight getting worse each year, certainly Alexander Gardner was his man.

Brady realized that Gardner, like himself, was a quiet, unassuming, extremely honest, hard worker. So Brady made Gardner a proposition. "Why not come to America and take charge of my gallery? As for the wet-plate process, we could try that and see how it works out, and see also how the public would take to it." The details of the arrangement have never been revealed. But it is known that Brady agreed to pay Gardner's fare to America.

So Brady's learning of the wet-plate process and his meeting with Alexander Gardner made his European trip a marked success. The silver medal from the Crystal Palace was nice to have. In time he would have many medals —but nothing so valuable as this new photographic process and his new partner, Gardner.

Chapter 8

Three New Galleries

Brady and Julia returned from Europe in May, 1852, rested and refreshed. They had been away almost a year and Brady was now quite ready to undertake something new. He was encouraged by the award of the silver medal at London and the fine reception he had received in Europe.

During his absence, the gallery under the supervision of the young Southerner George S. Cook had prospered. Cook was a fine photographer and the business had flourished. The gallery turned out as many as 30,000 portraits a year. Since Brady kept up his prices, these were not the cheap daguerreotypes which were at that time flooding the market.

America was growing. Prosperity was in the air.

Enterprise was on the march. Simple men of humble station, some of whom could barely read or write, were becoming millionaires. And Brady, a farm boy from upstate New York, was now on his way to fortune. The failure of his first Washington venture and the cost of his extended European trip did not trouble him in the least. He was now worth close to $100,000.

Brady decided it was now time to open a new gallery, the best and finest in New York. He found a good building at 359 Broadway, which had some large lofts. The fact that the street floor was occupied by Thompson's saloon did not deter him. Today socialites would hardly climb two or three flights of stairs to visit a photrographer's studio over a saloon. But in Brady's day there was little stigma attached to a saloon; Brady even advertised his new gallery as "over Thompson's saloon," for he was aware that New Yorkers knew the location of Thompson's better than the address 359 Broadway.

The opening of this splendid gallery was described in the New York papers as well as in *Humphrey's Journal*. The reception room, 40 feet long, was lighted by a fine chandelier with sparkling crystals and milk glass globes for the gas jets. Velvet drapes hung to the floor that was covered by a brightly patterned, rose-colored carpet. Lace curtains hung at the windows. There were rosewood chairs and comfortable benches, marble-top tables, a reception desk, and showcases for pictures, miniatures, and lockets. From the walls in gilt frames hung the famous Brady collection of the portraits of distinguished statesmen, poets, artists, gentlemen of noble birth, and ladies of great charm and elegance.

The retiring room, where ladies could comb their hair and make themselves beautiful before facing the camera, was decorated in green and gold; and the walls were covered with plate-glass mirrors. Then there were operating rooms, rooms for polishing plates, darkrooms, a chemical room, and storerooms for supplies and finished pictures.

All in all, Brady's new gallery was a show place, in 1853 the finest in New York. Brady continued to dress his part. He patronized excellent tailors for his black suits. He wore fine linen shirts, made to order for him, and a broad, brocaded silk scarf. His handkerchiefs were of the finest linen. He usually carried a cane, as did many fashionable gentlemen of the day.

Business was good. Great crowds poured into Brady's new gallery. Thus he was able, in the face of heavy competition, to keep up his prices. He was against cheap pictures and advertised in the New York papers to explain his position.

One advertisement read: "New York abounds with announcements of 25 cent and 50 cent Daguerreotypes. But little science, experience or taste is requisite to produce these, so called, cheap pictures. During several years that I have devoted to the Daguerreian Art, it has been my constant labor to perfect and elevate it. The result has been that the prize of excellence has been accorded to my pictures. . . wherever exhibited on either side of the Atlantic. Art has always suffered when the public have been deceived by unfounded assumptions of economy."

The advertisement then described his new gallery, which he had designed "for the production of first-class pictures." Brady was ready, however, to make a slight compromise so as not to lose extra business. For "such persons as may desire cheap likenesses, I take this opportunity of announcing that I am prepared to furnish Daguerreotypes at fifty cents and upward at my old establishment." The advertisement concluded, "I wish to vindicate true art, and leave the community to decide whether it is best to encourage real excellence or its opposite; to preserve and perfect an art, or permit it to degenerate by inferiority of materials which must correspond with the meanness of the price."

In the same year that Brady opened his new gallery, a buzz of excitement sounded throughout the American photographic scene. Attention was now concentrated on Archer's wet-plate process, which Brady had seen demonstrated in London and which his friend, the young Scotsman, Alexander Gardner, was so enthusiastic about. For some unknown reason, although Gardner had agreed to come to America and Brady had agreed to pay his passage, the Scotsman's journey was delayed. Gardner did not arrive in New York until three years later in 1856.

In the meantime, photographers in America were

experimenting with the wet-plate process. They followed the directions sent over from England, but the process was complicated and quite involved. Yet it presented great advantages and opened a new vista in photography.

Brady's friend, the former engineer and pupil of Morse, Edward Anthony, was one of the first photographers in America to make a print by using the wet-plate process. Anthony was most ingenious and not only experimented in photography, but also carried on a highly successful business supplying the trade with photographic materials, apparatus, chemicals, and studio equipment.

Then too, Whipple in Boston had gone into the wet-plate business in a big way. Whipple, it seems, obtained some patent rights from Archer to exploit this invention in America. But since everyone knew the full details of the process as it was reported in the journals, he had no great secrets he could trade. Whipple, however, soon made fine prints on paper and showed that he was the foremost master of this medium. Because of this success, many American photographers beat a path to his door to learn the fine points of his wet-plate technique. For this instruction Whipple charged a fee of $50.

Even Brady journeyed to Boston to visit Whipple in his studio. While he had seen the process demonstrated in London, it was certainly worth $50 to acquire some of the fine points. Brady could not afford to wait for Alexander Gardner to reach the United States. Even though he had never studied chemistry, here was something he would have to learn. A new photographic boom was on.

Brady could now see that daguerreotypes were doomed. The wet-plate process would soon replace them entirely.

Since the wet-plate process was to hold the center of the photographic stage for many years and since all the Civil War pictures, Brady's and those other photographers, were made by this process, it would be well to see what it was that Brady learned.

Here is a brief description of the process. First a glass plate, usually 8 inches by 10, was cleaned and polished to make it dust-free. Then a solution of guncotton in alcohol and ether, called collodion, was used to coat one side of the plate. The collodion was "floated on" to the plate as it was held by one corner. Care had to be taken that the thick fluid was "floated on" evenly so that there were no ripples. The plate then was set to dry in a rack. The trick was to let the ether and alcohol evaporate until the coating was of just the right degree of stickiness.

In the subdued orange light of the darkroom, while the coating on the plate was still very tacky, it was soaked for about five minutes in a bath of silver nitrate solution. The silver particles adhering to the collodion coating made the plate sensitive to light. When the plate turned a creamy yellow, it was taken out of the solution, drained, and while still wet placed in a plate holder that protected it from exposure by a lightproof slide.

The prepared plate was then placed in the camera. The plate had to be exposed in at least 25 minutes, or it would be spoiled. After exposure, the plate was returned to the darkroom and developed in a solution of sulfate of iron and acetic acid, and washed in a solution of potassium cyanide, a most deadly poison. This last solution removed the excess of silver from the surface image. The plate was finally dipped in iodized water and drained. Then, over a gentle flame, the plate was dried and, while still warm, varnished.

At no time in the entire process could one's fingers touch the glass surface. The plate had to be held by the edges. Handling a glass plate this way is quite a trick, especially when the plate is a large one; and some of Brady's plates were extremely large.

There were hazards with chemicals; hazards with emulsions that blistered, rippled, or made spots; hazards with contamination; too much heat or too much cold; too much breeze; dust; plates too wet or too dry. The process was very tricky; many plates got out of control and had to be discarded.

By the wet-plate process, Brady was soon making full-sized portrait heads, using glass plates 14 by 17 inches and even 17 by 20 inches. These he called "Imperial" photographs, and he sold them to New York's society at very fancy prices, $15 to $20. Brady's Imperials were at once the rage.

Now, at last, Brady had shaken off the cheap mob

[87]

of daguerreotype photographers. Imperials became his specialty. Soon his walls were covered with Imperials of America's distinguished men and women. Some of his plates he printed directly on canvas, and he then employed artists to finish them in oils, paying several hundred dollars for each picture.

When Gardner finally joined Brady in 1856, the newcomer was very much impressed with the Imperials and with Brady's artistry. Gardner lost no time in acquiring Brady's wet-plate technique. Now Brady was in a position to teach Gardner. Brady had known from the first that his young friend was a fine craftsman and chemist. Since he was also a fine photographer, Brady gave him full charge of his gallery so that Brady could have full time for experimenting and for organizing his ideas.

Before Gardner joined Brady in New York, far on the other side of the world events took place that fired Brady's imagination. This milestone in photography was not a new discovery but a new application. It proved a most dramatic one indeed. The camera had been used in the gallery, in the home, on the quiet landscape—it had even been trained on the moon. Now it went to war and set up its lens on the battle front!

The Crimean War had broken out between Russia and England and France. This was the war immortalized by Tennyson's "Charge of the Light Brigade," and it was in this war that Florence Nightingale distinguished herself as a nurse. But one more historic name should be added to those immortalized by the Crimean War: Roger Fenton.

Though a few daguerreotypes of the Mexican War late in the 1840's had been taken, Roger Fenton was the world's first real war photographer. He was the first to come under fire and record battle action. Fenton's difficulties and dangers were soon to become Brady's. In 1855 Fenton sailed from England, having carefully planned his expedition. He had had a small wagon built that he fitted up as a darkroom. He took with him five cameras, 700 glass plates, all the chemicals necessary for the wet-plate process, food, tools, and harness for horses. He bought his horses when the ship put in at Gibraltar. After his "photographic van" was put ashore in Turkey, he drove overland for a full month before he smelled gunpowder.

Fenton had some exciting experiences. While he was working in his van during one battle, part of the wagon roof was torn off by a shell. He was often in danger, but this did not deter him. He said that he suffered most from the heat, which was terrible. "When my van door is closed. . .perspiration is running down my face and dripping like tears. The developing solution is so hot I can hardly bear my hands in it."

He returned to London a few months later with 350 most dramatic and unusual plates. Many woodcuts were made from these photographs and at once reproduced in the *Illustrated London News* and other European magazines. Here was the real thing. Now for the first time the

[89]

camera was serving as both correspondent and historian. Here was the forerunner of a new kind of photography, photojournalism.

Once more Brady turned his face toward Washington. He had sworn that he would someday return. Now it was not only possible but very desirable.

Times had changed. The daguerreotype was fast withering on its dying vine. Competitors could no longer threaten him. The wet-plate process had given Brady his Imperials, a popular commodity that had captured all New York society. What it had done in New York it could also do in Washington.

Besides, there was Alexander Gardner, who not only knew chemistry and was a fine photographer, but had also a hidden talent of which Brady had been unaware. Gardner was an excellent accountant and business manager. Gardner was just the right man to be manager of his newly projected Washington gallery. Brady knew he was fortunate. He could not have found a better man, nor one more honest, efficient and loyal.

In 1856, Brady located his gallery in the heart of Washington on Pennsylvania Avenue, that joins the White House with the Capitol. The new gallery was not far from the fashionable National Hotel where he had lived before. It was close to the halls of government. The political clientele, which changed to some extent every time there was an election, would find a gallery close at hand.

This new gallery, with Gardner in charge, was a success from the very start. Gardner soon had more work than he could handle alone, and so he sent for his brother James to come from England and give him a helping hand. James lost no time crossing the ocean.

The reception room of Brady's Washington gallery was designed to attract the public. Situated on the second floor, it soon became a kind of public showplace, open daily except Sundays. On the walls hung oil paintings made from Brady's photographs and large photographs of famous people. There customers could see, large as life, pictures of James Fenimore Cooper, Washington Irving, Audubon, and the famous New York banker, Daniel Drew, as well as distinguished statesmen. From his New York gallery Brady brought to Washington an exquisite little picture done on porcelain of Mrs. August Belmont and a watercolor portrait of the famous American actress, Miss Maggie Mitchell.

For entertainment of the waiting patrons there was a large wooden box with stereoscopic views. Here were pictures Brady had made of European scenes, on his travels, views of Niagara Falls from every available angle, and a set of French comic pictures.

On the floor above the reception room was the finishing and mounting room. Here prints were retouched, tinted; and here many were finished in oils, crayon, or watercolor. Occasionally some were finished in india ink and shaded with charcoal.

[*91*]

The camera man worked on the top floor directly under the broad skylight. The operating room had two cameras, four headrests, and four posing chairs, including a small one for children. There were additional props: two tables, a plate-glass mirror, a marble stand, a clock, a foot rest, draperies, and painted backdrops. One of the large arm chairs was on loan from the House of Representatives to give dignity to the many public officials Brady photographed. This old chair was to become famous, for Brady photographed Abraham Lincoln many times as he sat in it.

From the top floor a ladder went up to the roof, where wooden racks held long lines of printing frames that in those days were exposed directly to the sun. Appointments for sittings were made only for the morning hours, from eight to twelve, because the light was best at that time. On rainy days all appointments were cancelled.

There is no record of what Gardner, as manager, or his brother James, was paid. But two assistant photographers, both experts, received $11 a day, and $16.66 if they had to work on Sunday. The women who did the tinting and mounting were paid only $8 a week. The gallery also employed a full-time bookkeeper and an errand boy.

The Washington gallery was to become of paramount importance in Brady's career. At first, since the gallery was in Gardner's capable hands, Brady only visited it occasionally. Sometimes he came to Washington because there were appointments with very important people. At other times he came to see if he could drum up business. But soon he and Julia moved to Washington. Once more they took rooms at the National Hotel.

Photographs recorded a faithful image, and the great illustrated weeklies were beginning to use them in recording current events. *Harper's Weekly* and *Leslie's Illustrated Newspaper,* two of the most progressive illustrated magazines in America, and the *Illustrated London News* and *L'Illustration* in Paris had in the past relied on artists to draw pictures of events the artists usually never saw. Now the illustrated papers got hold of photographs, which skillful wood engravers and lithographers could reproduce quite faithfully. In this way events of public interest—a fire, a railroad wreck, a coronation, a public funeral, a balloon ascension, a new machine, or anything else that was in the forefront of the news—could be reproduced with a faithfulness never before possible. Beneath the picture there was a credit line.

Brady immediately saw the value to be derived from such credit lines, and he began regularly supplying the illustrated magazines with anything he happened to photograph that had news value. Sometimes it was a portrait of a distinguished man; sometimes it was a scene or event. These pictures began appearing in almost every issue. The reader saw the credit lines to Brady. Understanding the value of publicity, Brady took care to see that his name was constantly before the American public.

In 1860, another event made photographic history. Two men, Professor Samuel King of Providence and the Boston photographer, J. W. Black, made a balloon ascension to take pictures over Boston. It was a hair-raising ride. Gas leaked from the bag of the balloon and spoiled some of the wet plates. The balloon was caught in wild wind currents. In the end, it landed in a tree, after having been in the air for more than two hours and travelling thirty miles. When the plates were developed, the two men had a real prize, a picture of Boston taken from the air, the first aerial photograph.

The picture was a sensation. The people of Boston looked at the picture and could hardly believe what they saw. Dr. Oliver Wendell Holmes, contributing editor of the *Atlantic Monthly,* wrote that the picture showed Boston "as the eagle and the wild goose see it."

During the 1850's, New York City grew rapidly. A great tide of immigration swelled over the shores of the United States during the decade, more than 2,500,000 persons. Most of the immigrants disembarked in New York. When Brady left for Europe in 1851, most of the city's activity had been below Canal Street. Washington Square was considered quite uptown. But by 1860, Washington Square had already become a fashionable residential section.

The rapid growth in population brought overcrowding and tenement districts. People were pushed uptown, and where the people moved, business followed.

The old entertainment center on the Bowery moved to Astor Place and 14th Street. The most popular play of the decade, *Uncle Tom's Cabin,* put a flame under the issue of slavery.

Great newspapers flourished, led by Greeley's *Tribune* and Bennett's *Herald.* Together they had a greater circulation than all of the papers printed in the South combined. The weekly edition of the *Tribune* went, 176,-000 strong, by mail to homes in the North and West across the country. Brady knew both Greeley and Bennett and had witnessed their rise to great power. Reporters of both papers visited Brady's galleries regularly. The photographer understood the problems of news gathering and the value of publicity. He remained friendly with both rival newspapers and often supplied them with photographs of news value. The credit line "From a Photograph by Brady" appeared often, thus carrying his name not only to New Yorkers and Washingtonians, but all over the world. And his name appeared still more often in the illustrated weeklies than in the newspapers.

Brady moved with the city, the original Fulton Street gallery going up Broadway near to Bleeker Street. And in 1860, Brady decided to move his fashionable gallery "over Thompson's saloon," which specialized in his Imperials. He found a suitable location at Broadway and 10th Street, directly opposite the fashionable Grace Church and very close to the new and glamorous department store of his old employer, A. T. Stewart.

Brady spared no expense in making this 10th Street gallery the showplace of America, the most magnificent of all galleries. For elegance, it had no rivals in all America and Europe. Its carpets, crystal chandeliers, the very latest heating equipment, overstuffed furniture—all were the finest money could buy. Pictures of famous people covered the walls. There were special dressing rooms, large camera rooms, darkrooms, and vast lofts for making enlargements and oil paintings. A private "ladies entrance" led directly to the operating rooms to accomodate those clients arriving in costume who wished to avoid passing through the often crowded lounge.

The operating rooms had skylights designed by Brady much larger than in any other gallery and made of tinted glass. Brady had found that tinted glass gave a more agreeable light than plain glass. The expanded size allowed him to reduce the time of exposure.

Brady's name was now so well known over the country that it became a household word as Bret Harte indicated in his poem, "Her Letter":

> *Well, yes—if you saw us out driving*
> *Each day in the Park, four-in-hand*
> *If you saw poor mama contriving*
> *To look supernaturally grand.—*
> *If you saw papa's picture, as taken*
> *By Brady, and tinted at that—*
> *You'd never suspect he sold bacon*
> *And flour at Poverty Flat.*

Brady was now proprietor of three highly profitable photographic studios, the most profitable and the most fashionable in the United States. He was now worth more than $100,000. He invested some of his money in oil wells and silver mines and in uptown lots near Central Park. He had a feeling that the population of New York would continue to grow, thus forcing people to move still farther uptown. He was right.

In 1857 had begun the great wave of popularity of the carte de visite, a small photograph about the size of a visiting card that became a substitute for it. This little photograph, about two inches by three, had a sudden and sensational vogue, beginning in France, moving to England, and then quickly to America. The pictures were usually taken eight on one plate and all eight printed at one time. Then they were cut apart and mounted on small stiff cards that often had a gilt edge.

Photographers could not keep up with the demand for the cartes de visite. People had themselves photographed and ordered dozens. Many hallways had trays and baskets filled with cartes de visite left by callers. A great popular demand for the photographs of notables on these small cards also arose. Photographers were busy taking pictures of actors and actresses, circus performers, freaks, prizefighters, weight lifters, gentlemen of high station, newsboys, statesmen—every conceivable kind of popular hero. In fact, everybody who was anybody had his picture on this popular small card.

In England a week after Albert, the Prince Consort, died, 70,000 pictures of him were sold. In America a thousand prints a day were sold of Major Robert Anderson after his heroic defense of Fort Sumter.

Brady had a vast collection of photographs of famous people in America. No gallery in the country was better equipped to meet this fresh onrush of business. His assistants copied many of his pictures in the small popular size. But Brady had more carte de visite business than he could take care of. He therefore entered into a partnership with his good friend Edward Anthony of Anthony and Company. The Company could undertake the wholesale manufacture of these small prints. As fast as Brady and his men could copy old pictures, the plates went off to Anthony and Company. Brady received $4,000 a year for the use of his negatives and a share in the profit from sale of the cards.

But Brady did not wholly like this business because it was too commercial. Turning out the pictures required little skill or artistry. This contract for the production of the popular cards was Brady's first business venture with Anthony and Company. Later on, as we shall see, Anthony and Company had other business arrangements with Brady, and at one time they extended Brady unlimited credit for photographic supplies.

Prophets
and a Prince

HARRIET BEECHER STOWE,
LYMAN AND HENRY WARD BEECHER

EDWARD, PRINCE OF WALES, (sixth from right) AND HIS ENTOURAGE

Chapter 9

A Backwoods Lawyer and a Prince

In February, 1860, just about a month after Brady had opened his 10th Street gallery, Abraham Lincoln came to New York City. He had had an invitation to speak at the Plymouth Church in Brooklyn, but some members of the Young Men's Central Republican Union of New York City had persuaded him to speak at Cooper Union instead.

One of these "young men" was the poet, William Cullen Bryant, co-owner and editor of the New York *Evening Post*. This "young man" was 65 years old in 1860. Another "young man," age 49, who had urged this change to Cooper Union was Horace Greeley. Both Bryant and Greeley were friends of Brady.

The backwoods lawyer, Lincoln, was known in the

West, where his debates with Stephen A. Douglas in the 1858 Illinois senatorial campaign had been sensational. But Lincoln had never spoken before in New York, and it was very doubtful in many people's minds whether this self-made lawyer—risen from a log cabin, awkward, unpolished, and bearing the stamp of his origins—would be at all acceptable to the sophisticated East. There tradition, culture, education, and polished manners were important. How could the East accept a crude backwoods lawyer?

When Lincoln arrived in New York, he went straight to the Astor House to meet Richard C. McCormick, who had charge of the arrangements. James D. Horan in his biography of Mathew Brady, tells of this meeting: "A giant of a man opened the door. McCormick was taken aback when he saw him. He later recalled that the Illinois lawyer, 'half alligator, half horse,' was wearing a cheap black suit, 'much wrinkled from the careless packing in the valise. His form and manner were indeed very odd, and we thought him the most unprepossessing public man we had ever met.'"

As they walked down the street together, Lincoln suddenly saw an old acquaintance from Illinois. They shook hands and the man told Lincoln that he had lost $100,000 since he had last seen him. "Lincoln grinned. 'Well, I have eight thousand in the bank, the Springfield cottage, and if they make me Vice-President with Seward I'll increase it to twenty thousand and that is as much as any man ought to ask.'" (After the Cooper Union speech, Lincoln began to feel differently about what a man ought to ask.)

McCormick and Lincoln went on. At length they arrived at Brady's studio. Roy Meredith in *Mr. Lincoln's Camera Man* gives an interesting account of the sitting: "After introductions, Brady began arranging the apparatus. . . . Brady studied his subject as he adjusted his camera. . . ." He saw him much as Lincoln's Danville, Illinois, law partner, Ward Hill Lamon, described him. Lincoln was over six feet tall—six feet four to be exact, but his legs were out of proportion to his body. He had large ears, a blunt nose, a thick upper lip, a protruding and sharp chin, flabby cheeks, wrinkled skin, and his Adam's apple was large and protruding. Added to all this, his serious and sad expression showed that he was weighed down with care and suffering.

Such was the Lincoln that now confronted Brady. What could he do with such a subject? He studied the problem before him. As Brady later recalled, "I had great trouble in making a natural picture. When I got him before the camera, I asked him if I might not arrange his collar, and with that he began to pull it up. 'Ah,' said Lincoln, 'I see you want to shorten my neck.' 'That's just it,' I answered, and we both laughed." Brady took the picture, one that was to become very famous.

Lincoln's Cooper Union speech that evening defined his position on slavery and was a tremendous success. He closed with the immortal words, "Let us have faith that right makes might, and in that faith, let us, to the end, dare do our duty as we understand it." Next morning Horace Greeley's *Tribune* gave the speech five columns, printing every word of it. Lincoln's words had a ring of deep sincerity and conviction. He appealed to reason and man's good sense. He did not propose that the evil of slavery be exterminated at once. But he did propose that slavery should not be extended into the new territories of the growing nation.

Many people across the nation had asked the question: "Who is Abraham Lincoln?" Now they had their answer, and they knew exactly where he stood.

The day after the speech, Brady had a great demand for his photograph of that backwoods lawyer who was wearing "a cheap wrinkled suit." The press wanted pictures. They made woodcuts and printed them with the well known credit line: "Photograph by Brady." This was the first of many pictures that Brady made of Lincoln, and it went all over the United States. The following May Lincoln was nominated as the Republican candidate for President.

Some time later, after Lincoln had been elected President but before he was inaugurated, he came to have Brady take his picture again. When the sitting was over Ward Hill Lamon said, "I have not introduced you to Brady." Lincoln replied, "Brady and the Cooper Union speech made me President."

In the fall of 1860, Brady added a prince to his

famous portrait gallery. The eldest son of Queen Victoria, heir to the British throne, was Edward, Prince of Wales, later at 61 to become King Edward VII. In 1860 he was handsome, charming, had winning manners, and he was young—only 19. He won the hearts of the people. The young prince and his entourage of a dozen or so statesmen and titled aristocrats came to the United States after visiting Canada. In New York they took rooms at the Fifth Avenue Hotel. All New York was determined to make the prince welcome.

There were parades; the whole fire department came out in his honor; there were fireworks at night; and bands played in front of the hotel. In his honor New York society gave a "Diamond Ball"; it was five o'clock in the morning before the Prince and his royal party got back to their hotel.

Meanwhile the New York photographers were all wondering who would have the honor of photographing the Prince and his party. Many tried to find some connection, social or political, which might lead to an introduction. But Brady made no such effort.

Suddenly one day a messenger came to Brady's studio; the photographer was invited to come to the Fifth Avenue Hotel the next morning at ten o'clock to meet the Prince and talk over arrangements for photographing his entire party. Brady was on time for his appointment. The Prince said that he and his party could come to Brady's studio at noon that same day and that they would then be glad to see his work and pose for their pictures.

The Prince, however, did ask one small favor of Brady. Since the royal presence always drew large, enthusiastic crowds, would it be possible for Brady to close the doors of his gallery to the public during this visit? In this way they would not be interrupted. Brady readily consented to this request.

Hurrying back to his studio, Brady ordered the doors closed to the public. Then he went upstairs and made things ready. His assistants started cleaning glass plates. Chemicals were made ready; camera lenses were polished bright; and all details were attended to. Now and then Brady's people would look out of the windows to see if the royal carriages were approaching. Brady and his assistants watched the avenue and watched the clock.

At last! At twelve-thirty the carriages came into sight. Immediately crowds gathered. The carriages stopped at the "Ladies' Entrance," which led directly to Brady's operating rooms. As the Prince stepped out of his carriage, he acknowledged the cheers of the crowd by tipping his tall silk hat. He wore gray flannel trousers and the coat that was named after his father, Prince Albert, Queen Victoria's husband. When the Prince tipped his hat to the crowd, they saw a handsome head of brown curly hair. In his hand, the Prince carried a dark bamboo cane.

When the Prince and his party had climbed the stairs, they found Brady waiting to show them through his gallery. The royal party paused to examine and admire many of the portraits on the walls, calling out the names of those they recognized.

Brady took several pictures of the entire group, together with the Prince. Then he took several full-length pictures of the Prince alone, and a number of pictures of small groups, some with the Prince and some without him.

One incident during the royal visit became legend. While Brady's doors were closed to the public, one very old gentleman did manage somehow to get into the gallery. Brady's assistants were about to put him out when Brady stopped them so that he could ask the old man to explain his presence. The old man said that before he migrated to America, he had been a servant in the royal household in England when the Prince was born. Now he only wanted to see him once more.

This touching request Brady gladly granted. When the picture taking was over, Brady told the Prince about the old man. The Prince, with great courtesy, came forward and shook the old man's hand. The smile on the old man's face was unforgettable.

Before the royal party departed, Brady turned to the Duke of Newcastle and said, "Your Grace, might I ask to what I owe your favor to my studio? I am at a loss to understand your kindness."

The Duke replied, "Are you not Mr. Brady who earned the prize nine years ago in London? You owe it to yourself. We had your place of business down in our notebooks before we started."

Brady escorted the royal party to their carriages. The

police were on hand to clear a path through the vast crowd. The Prince expressed his pleasure and gratitude, and before stepping into his carriage he shook hands with Brady, as did each member of the party.

As a memento of this visit the Prince sent Mrs. Brady a small elegant writing box made of ebony and inlaid with mother-of-pearl. To Brady he sent a handsome walking stick made of Honduran rosewood with a fine ivory handle mounted over a gold band on which was engraved, "M. B. Brady from Edward Prince of Wales." The Prince also sent Brady a gold ring. Brady was very fond of this walking stick and carried it constantly. He also wore the ring to remind him of the happy occasion of the Prince's visit.

Chapter 10

The Brooding Conflict

S hortly after the Prince's visit to Brady's gallery, Lincoln was elected President. Brady could feel the tension in the air. The Southern states began to secede. History was about to explode, and Brady knew that he should be in Washington. He lost no time. He and Julia packed at once and moved to Washington, back to their old home, the National Hotel. This was to be their residence for a good many years to come.

Lincoln arrived in the capital on February 23, 1861, after the long journey from Springfield, Illinois, a journey marked by many speeches along the route. In Baltimore, where he had to cross the city to change trains, there had been a plot against his life. As protection, Allan Pinkerton, the detective, accompanied him, as well as his old friend Ward Hill Lamon. In Washington, rooms had been reserved for him at the Willard Hotel. He went there for breakfast. He excused himself and retired to his room. That afternoon he and his friend Ward Hill Lamon went to Brady's studio. They needed another picture, one to show the Lincoln who would soon be inaugurated as President of the United States.

Lincoln seemed different. Since Brady had taken the last photograph, Lincoln had grown a beard, as was the fashion of the day.

As Meredith tells it, Brady had asked the artist George H. Story, who had a studio in the same building as his gallery, to come in and help pose Lincoln. "When Story walked in, Lincoln and Lamon had already arrived, and Lincoln was seated at a table waiting to be posed. . . . His depression was manifest, but he said nothing to expose his thoughts." Story later noted that, "He did not utter a word, and he seemed absolutely indifferent to all that was going on about him; and he gave the impression that he was a man who was overwhelmed with anxiety and fatigue and care."

Brady was not sure that this was the correct appearance for a picture of the future President, especially considering the troubled times. But Story said, "Bring the camera at once." This was no time for tact or pretense. "Honesty was written in every line of his face," said Story. That is exactly how Brady and his assistants photographed him. And this photograph is now history.

Before the inauguration Brady photographed Mrs.

Lincoln in her full pink silk dress trimmed with flowers and lace, the dress she would be wearing at the Inaugural Ball.

Two days before the Inauguration, Brady went to see his friend General Meigs, who had charge of the construction of the unfinished Capitol before which the ceremony would be held. He asked permission to set up his camera at a good location and to make photographs of the Inauguration. Permission was granted.

Early in the morning of the Inaugural Day, Brady and Gardner set up their camera and the little tent that served them as a darkroom to prepare their wet plates. Then they waited. The crowd gathered.

Old Chief Justice Taney, whom Brady had photographed in his Washington gallery, administered the oath of office, the ninth time he had sworn in a President. As soon as the oath had been administered the new President read his Inaugural Address. Brady and Gardner heard the close of it, imploring for peace between the North and South: "I am loath to close. We are not enemies but friends. We must not be enemies. Though passion may have strained, it must not break our bonds of affection."

When the speech was ended, Brady and Gardner packed up their equipment and hurried back to the studio to develop their plates. Many engravings of these pictures were made and reproduced in newspapers and magazines so that people all over the United States could see what the Inauguration in Washington looked like.

But the cleavage between the North and South could

no longer be bridged with words. In April Fort Sumter was bombarded by Confederate guns. It was war! Lincoln called for 75,000 volunteers for three months. He thought that that would be enough time to get things settled. Volunteers answered the call all over the North, and regiments began pouring into Washington to protect the capital and defend the Union. Everyday there were parades on Pennsylvania Avenue. In a few weeks the city was overcrowded.

The carte de visite craze, which had subsided, burst forth anew. Everybody needed a picture of himself in uniform, taken in Washington, to send back home. Working day and night, Brady and his assistants tried to fill the hundreds of orders for the little cartes de visite, which were so handy to slip into an envelope and send to Pa and Ma, Auntie and Uncle, the latest girl, and the old ones too. With pictures, no letter had to be sent. Brady's business was more profitable than ever before.

Brady could see that the troops of both sides would soon be moving into battle positions. The time was drawing near when war in all its fury would be breaking loose. There would be action, adventure, and danger. History would be a hot furnace. Before his eyes history would be made. This was no time for mere cartes de viste. Brady felt that he had something more important on which to train his camera lens.

His mind was made up. He decided to get on the field of battle. To this end Brady began making plans. He would need a horse and wagon to move all his plates and chemicals. He knew that Roger Fenton, who had gone to the Crimean War, had had a wagon which served him as a moving darkroom. So Brady began designing one that would fit his needs.

One thing more he also needed: permission from someone in high authority. Civilians are not tolerated on a field of battle. But somehow he was determined to go. Fortunately Brady knew people in power. He decided to use his influence. "I felt I had to go," said Brady later. "A spirit in my feet said 'go' and I went."

First he visited old General Winfield Scott, who at 75 was in command of the Army. Brady had long known General Scott, to whom he had often brought wild ducks for his dinner table. Now, on this visit, the General shook his head and confessed that permission to go on the battle field was out of his power; he was soon to be replaced by a younger officer. "General McDowell will succeed me tomorrow. You will have difficulty, but he and Colonel Whipple are the ones for you to see."

Brady was not able to see McDowell; he was not in Washington, but somewhere with his troops. In the meantime, while Brady waited, he continued to work on his darkroom wagon. Then one day he went to see Allan Pinkerton, who had now taken it upon himself to act as a oneman secret service agency. Pinkerton took Brady to Lincoln. Here was the chance Brady had been waiting for. He lost no time in disclosing his plan for photographing the Civil War in action.

Pinkerton said he would have no objection provided

Brady was careful and did not get in the way of any military maneuvers. Lincoln was silent. He smiled and wrote two words on a paper that he signed and handed to Brady. The two words read: "Pass Brady."

HOUSE
DIVIDED

*Brady
Photographic Van
in the Field*

Lincoln Meets McClellan in the Field

GENERAL ROBERT E. LEE

GENERAL PHIL SHERIDAN

The Dead after Fredericksburg

GEN. R. B. POTTER AND STAFF—
and BRADY, *right*

MRS. JOHN SLIDELL

The Fairy Wedding Group.

Entered according to Act of Congress in the year 1863 by M.B. Brady in the Clerks Office of the District Court for the So District of New York

GEORGE WASHINGTON (*Commodore*) McNUTT, CHARLES S. (*General Tom Thumb*) STRATTON, MRS. CHARLES S. STRATTON (*née Lavinia Warren*), MINNIE WARREN

Chapter 11

Brady's What's-it Wagon

The wagon that Brady built to use on the field of battle was a strange-looking affair, like nothing anyone had ever seen before. It was built on a buggy frame with four wheels; but it was covered with canvas cloth and looked something like a small sawed-off covered wagon—the kind used by settlers of the West.

Seeing this strange contraption for the first time, soldiers would look at each other with a questioning glance. "What is it?" they asked. No one knew. No one could answer. So in a very short time the familiar wagon —for Brady was here and there and everywhere that any action was brewing—became known as the "What's-it Wagon."

A step at the back of the wagon led up to a canvas

curtain that covered the entrance to the traveling darkroom. Inside, the white canvas was lined with black cloth so that the interior would be completely light proof. The wagon floor was sunk below the axle to hold the deep tanks of chemicals. The operator stood up, his head almost touching the top of the canvas, while he dipped the plates, first to coat them, then to sensitize them before putting them on the rack to dry. After the plates were exposed, they were dipped in the developer, fixing, and washing solutions. The whole procedure was carried on in almost total darkness. A small candle in a deep red lantern provided the only light. Darkness was not the only difficulty. The working space was so small that the air was charged with the strong smell of the chemicals and the fumes made the operator's eyes smart. The sun beating down on the canvas added stifling heat to the fume-charged air and made it hard for the operator to breathe.

To top it all off, the white-canvas covered wagon made a conspicuous target. Rifle fire and shrapnel could easily tear asunder the light construction. All in all, with its deadly chemicals and hundreds of glass plates, the "What's-it Wagon" was a very dangerous place to be in when the firing started.

Yet Brady and his men were to find themselves many times working in this mobile darkroom under fire. Often they could not move the wagon to a safer place, for the exposed plates had to be developed at once or they would be ruined. At first, working under such conditions seemed worrisome. But in time Brady and his men got used to it, absorbed as they were in their work; and at last they came to pay less and less attention to discomfort and danger. Brady once said that when the War came on, he knew it was his destiny to make the camera into an instrument of history. He knew James Gordon Bennett had made a sensational paper of the *Herald*. He knew Horace Greeley had made the *Tribune* into a great newspaper. He knew the power and attraction of *Harper's Weekly* and *Leslie's Illustrated Newspaper*. He knew that a newspaper or magazine is great because of its reporting. But words make up only one kind of reporting. Pictures too can tell a story and often much better than words.

"I felt like a great newspaper," Brady said. "And I will have my men here and there and everywhere. They will cover the War. And the full story of the War will be told in pictures."

One wagon, he knew, would not be enough, and so after one was constructed, another was begun. And then another and another.

Brady was not the only person who had the idea of photographing the Civil War. As he was building his "What's-it Wagons" and gathering together supplies and training more assistants, the editor of the *American Journal of Photography,* though not taking the war too seriously, thought that perhaps here was a fresh opportunity for the photographer: "A battle scene is a fine subject for an artist—painter, historian or photographer.

We hope to see a photograph of the next battle. . . . There will be little danger in the active duties, for the photographer must be beyond the smell of gunpowder or his chemicals will not work."

Little did the editor know the extent of the dangers. Nor did he realize how thoroughly Brady was organizing his war project and that he and his assistants would be ready to risk their lives to save their plates.

At this early date, Brady had already arranged for the use of his battle-action pictures with *Harper's Weekly* and *Leslie's Illustrated Newspaper*.

When the warm weather came, everything seethed to a boil. Both politicians and the press cried for action, demanding that the Union Army march on Richmond, the Confederate capital, and that the South be taught a lesson. Union officers, however, felt that their Army was not yet ready for combat. The men had been hurriedly assembled; they were green and untrained; and the different branches were still uncoordinated. But the heat and the pressure were on. The cry was taken up: "On to Richmond!"

Many people in the North felt that the odds in their favor were overwhelming. The Union had more men and more supplies. Many people figured that taking Richmond was merely a matter of taking a little picnic ride into Virginia. Union soldiers were gay as they marched off from Washington "as though bound for a clambake," as one Northern newspaper put it.

Civilian men and women followed the Army just to see the fun of battle. Parties rode in carriages carrying lunchboxes and liquid refreshments. The livery stables of Washington ran out of horses and carriages to hire out. Everything that could move was rented. A vast crowd, a picnic of giant proportions, followed the Army into Virginia.

Now was the time for Brady to go into action. Here is the story in Brady's own words: "I went to the battle of Bull Run with two wagons from Washington. My personal companions were Dick McCormic, then a newspaper writer, Ned Hause and Al Waud, the sketch artist. We stayed all night at Centreville; we got as far as Blackburne's Ford; we made pictures and expected to be in Richmond the next day, but it was not so. . . ." This was the first surprise of the War, a war destined to be filled with many surprises.

When Brady reached the place where he thought the battle would be fought, he drew his wagon to the side and set up his cameras in a place commanding a good view. When the battle began, he started making his pictures. But then came the surprise. McDowell with a Union force of 30,000 was sure he could advance toward Richmond. For the greater part of the day, the Union troops were successful. In another hour, they felt, victory would surely be theirs. But the Confederate forces managed to join each other, and by three o'clock in the afternoon there was a decided turn in the battle. Thomas J. Jackson won his nickname "Stonewall."

The Southern army that had seemed on the verge of collapse now took the offensive and turned the tide of battle to a victorious rout of the Union Army. They were forced into a rapid retreat that soon became a disorderly and confused rout.

In the sudden rush to get back to Washington, all was confusion. The picnicking ladies and gentlemen were no help at all. Their carriages and horses blocked the roads. Many carriages were wrecked; many were commandeered to carry away the wounded. In the smashing, tumbling rush, heavy gun carriages pulled by galloping horses tore through everything, leaving a trail of wreckage behind.

The soldiers reached Washington before many of the footsore sightseeers. One Congressman's fine carriage returned with its Negro driver but without the Congressman, who was captured by the enemy. One Washington gentleman, Judge McCook, came back in a cart that also bore his wounded 17-year old son, whom he had picked up on the battlefield.

The picture, as recorded by Margaret Leech is complete and devastating: "On the banks of Bull Run, more had been lost than the battle, more than pride and honor. The tradition of Lexington had suffered an eclipse. . . . Gallant hearts were not enough. . . . American volunteers had been whipped, and shamefully whipped, and the country's blame fell heavily on their officers. Many of them had been among the first to run."

Many boys, after only this brief encounter, had had

[*128*]

enough of war and started home. Two hundred Union officers resigned. They had not expected war to be anything at all like this. The night after the battle the barrooms in the city of Washington were filled. Many heads were bandaged but everyone was drinking to forget—to forget defeat, to forget the face of sudden death, to forget that sickening sight of battle. War was no picnic.

Walt Whitman, the poet, saw this and wrote: "There you are shoulder-straps. But where are your companies? Where are your men? . . . Sneak, blow, put on airs there in Willard's sumptuous parlors and bar-rooms, or anywhere—no explanation will save you. Bull Run is your work. . . ."

This was Bull Run, but where was Brady?

Bull Run was Brady's first experience on the field of battle. As he himself recorded, he went out with two wagons. The battle began and he started taking pictures. Then the rout began. He took one or two pictures of this wild retreat. Then the wagon he was in overturned and the horse took fright and ran away. In the meantime the driver of his other wagon had taken cover in a sheltered grove.

Brady himself was forced to take to the woods. There for three days he wandered about with stragglers. At length he ran into a group of New York Fire Department Zouaves dressed in their colorful red bloomer trousers and Turkish jackets. Some of the men recognized "Brady of Broadway," and they gave him a sword belt and a long sword to defend himself with if necessary.

In this condition, tired, sore, hungry, but wearing a big sword under his linen duster, Brady got back to Washington. The Union army had its defeat. And Brady had his. But all was not lost. Nor was he discouraged. The next week he managed to locate his second wagon and save what he could of his own wrecked "What's-it Wagon." He even found his runaway horse. To make up for everything, the plates that were saved were splendid and unlike anything ever before photographed in America.

Brady now realized that Lincoln and people in the North had been over-optimistic when they felt that they needed soldiers for only three months. Brady himself had, like the others, thought that everything would surely be over in three months, or at least in six. He had figured that he could afford to put 20 men in the field and keep them supplied for the full six months. But now he had his doubts. This was a stubborn enemy.

Somehow he felt it would be a long war. It would take all the money he could get together to see it through. And it would be a bloody war, a hard and ugly conflict, more devastating than any war had ever been before. The dead, he felt, would mount to an unbelievable number. Brady was right.

Even the photographic journals now realized that war was no picnic. The editor of *Humphrey's Journal* was full of praise for Brady, for his courage and also for his pictures. "The public is indebted to Brady, of Broadway," he wrote, "for numerous excellent views of 'grim-visaged war.' He has been in Virginia with his camera and many and spirited are the pictures he has taken. His are the only reliable records of Bull Run. The correspondents of the Rebel newspapers are sheer falsifiers; the correspondents of the English press are altogether worse than either; but Brady never misrepresents. . . . This collection is the most curious and interesting we have ever seen. . . . Considering the circumstances under which they were taken, amidst the excitement, the rapid movements, and the smoke of the battlefield, there is nothing to compare with them in their powerful contrasts of light and shade."

Only a month or so before, the editor of the *American Journal of Photography* had ventured to say mildly that "We hope to see a photograph of the next battle." Now his hope was fully realized. But he hardly expected war to be so horrible, so grim. Now the photographer was away from the protection of his studio. He was out in the open. He was himself a target.

Then the editor, after seeing Brady's pictures, wrote, "The irrepressible photographer, like the warhorse, snuffs the battle from afar."

The photographer must go forward into the thick of the action; otherwise he will have no picture. He cannot delay, for no battle is ever repeated to accommodate a tardy photographer.

Chapter 12

Brady's Camera Records History

Wa ar always produces the unexpected. Surprise has ever been part of military strategy. Some surprises in war are thus intentional, designed to upset the enemy. But many of the surprises of war happen without planning and are unforeseen accidents. Other surprises were soon to come after Bull Run. The horses that drew Brady's "What's-it Wagons" were battle shy. The smell of gunpowder was unfamiliar to them and the sudden burst of shells made them jump with fright. Occasionally a wagon was overturned, or a sudden jolt caused by the frightened animals spilled the chemicals in the tanks and broke the glass plates.

Such accidents with the resultant losses multiplied as Brady, determined to cover the whole theatre of war, added more "What's-it Wagons" and assistants. He had his heart set on recording the full history of the War. He knew that history to be vital must be recorded at the moment it occurs. The day after the event, history is already cold and distorted. Brady said, "I had men in all parts of the army, like a great newspaper."

Brady spent vast sums of money to build this necessary network. It was a time for action, not economy. His friends in Anthony and Company gave him unlimited supplies on credit. He employed over 20 photographers. Within a year after the Battle of Bull Run, which had included every possible discouragement to any photographer, Brady had established 35 bases of operation.

Some of Brady's bases were rented shacks, others were log cabins, or temporary shelters put together with poles or a few boards and covered over with tarpaulins or tar paper. He used these places as stations to store supplies: chemicals, plates, extra cameras and other photographic equipment, as well as emergency rations for the operators and feed and bedding for the horses. Finished plates were often kept in these stations until it was convenient to collect them and take them safely to the Washington studio.

Brady studied maps and picked the points for his depots very carefully. He had to guess the route that the war would probably follow and choose his spots so that they would be convenient, accessible, and not too far apart. An operator forced by the tide of battle to abandon one station would then be able to have access to another, whether in advance or in retreat.

The whole plan, which Brady worked out carefully, had to be flexible. To keep 35 depots fully supplied and ready at all times required a fine talent for organization. He alone was his own commander-in-chief, his own board of strategy, and his own tactician. Instead of receiving funds from Congress, he had to do his own financing.

In this work he was greatly encouraged by the popularity of his truly unique "war views," which aroused great interest. He hoped, of course, later to sell reproductions of these pictures through his studios.

The studios in the meantime were helping to pay the expenses of his great enterprise. In the New York studio alone an average of over 200 portraits a month were taken during the Civil War years. The Washington gallery made a yearly profit of $12,000 dollars, besides the $4,000 dollars it received annually from the Anthony Company for the use of Brady plates.

After a battle, plates would be delivered to the Washington studio and prints quickly made. Word was soon circulated through the city, by word of mouth or through the press, that Brady already had pictures of the encounter recently reported in the newspapers.

One typical newspaper notice is recorded in *Mr. Lincoln's Camera Man*: "Mr. Brady has done something to bring home to us the terrible reality and earnestness of war. If he has not brought bodies and laid them in our dooryards and along the streets, he has done something very much like it. . . . Crowds of people are constantly going up the stairs; follow them, and you will find them bending over photographic views of the fearful battle field taken immediately after the action."

Brady and his "What's-it Wagons" followed the troops on their march. Brady and his men were in the rear with the army supply wagons. When the army's heavy wagons of supplies became stuck in the mud, Brady's wagon sometimes bogged down too. But often, since his wagons were very light, almost like a buggy or small butcher's wagon, the driver got out and maneuvered the horse off the road and ahead of the mired vehicles. In this way Brady or his assistants were often able to get through when the supplies and heavy cannon were at a standstill. War is filled with surprises.

Brady knew that his wagons had to travel light to be maneuverable. He had to have extra supplies on hand, for if one wagon was blown apart and all lost, without emergency supplies there could be no pictures of the imminent battle. The pictures were important because the pictures were history. And history does not wait. Because of this his wagons often operated in pairs.

When Brady reached the field where action was taking place, he had, of course, to keep out of the firing range and if possible find a sheltered place to tie up his horse and wagon. Then he would venture out on the field to make a survey, but one quite different from that an army officer would make. The officer would look for the enemy and see how, with what forces he had, he could gain the advantage. Brady needed no advantage in human lives. What he looked for was entirely different. He had no military eye. But he had the eye of an artist, the eye that understood human values, the eye for drama, and the eye for history. He was looking for an honest record of the event.

Often he had to wait until the action was over, or nearly over. This was usually in the late afternoon. By this time the boys usually had had enough fighting and were willing to quit for the day, to come together to reorganize their ranks, and to think of food. It was then that Brady and his assistants could venture out upon the field and set up their cameras. Though the action of the day was already over the field often told its own story. Some of those who had been killed outright were still lying on the ground. Those who had been slightly wounded and had managed to get to some aid station were now returning to their companies. Some of those who had been seriously wounded were at this moment being removed from the battlefield; some were still waiting for the overworked stretcher-bearers.

What remained on the field—cannon, debris, blasted wagons and horses, dead men, rifles, blown-off hats and shoes, smoking potholes—all this was the evidence of battle. All this waited for Brady's camera.

The field of battle once recorded, Brady and his men turned their cameras on the soldiers who had finished their day's work. They were hardly in the mood for picture taking, and Brady knew this. They had been through hell and their faces were grim. But when they saw this little, five-and-a-half-foot, redheaded Irishman with his blond pointed beard approach in his flowing linen duster and old straw hat, they sat up and took notice.

"Look what's coming," one might say.

"What's he carrying? One of those new 500-a-minute rattle guns?"

"Naw. It's a camera!"

Then another might call out, "We're gonna have a picture took. What do you know!"

"We're all heroes," called another. "Now we got to watch the birdie."

In the meantime, without delay, Brady had his camera in position and was looking about to see how he could possibly get the boys to sit still. If his eye caught one of the officers, in a pleasant quiet voice he might say, "Major, could you ask your men to stay quiet while I take their picture?"

The major usually took it all as a joke and would call out, "Men. Hold still for a moment or two. Your picture is wanted for your sweethearts."

Then one would say, "That's Brady and his 'What's-it Wagon.' I had my picture took by him at Bull Run."

"And it showed you running like the devil was after you," said another.

"I was not."

In the meantime Brady took out his watch and called, "Ready, men!"

The boys straightened up and struck a rigid pose,

trying to look half statue and half hero.

Removing the cap from the lens, Brady cried, "Steady now . . . There—it is all done! Thank you, men."

Losing no time, for the sun was now on its way down, Brady folded up his tripod and lifting his heavy camera onto his shoulder ran on to the next group where the same performance and much of the same conversation was repeated.

That is how Brady and his men took his pictures. They were taken here and there on every battle front and anywhere at all where there was action. To record a list of all the places that Brady covered would present a full chronology and most of the place names of the entire Civil War. The pictures themselves give this record. Words are unnecessary. And the record before us today remains undying.

In 1862, Brady had recorded the terrible slaughter at the battle of Antietam where 100,000 men took part and 500 pieces of artillery blasted away for 14 hours. His pictures were startling and almost unbelievable. But they were true, accurate, and filled with the grim and shocking reality of the horror of war.

Dr. Oliver Wendell Holmes, who had earlier praised the aerial photograph of Boston, came to this scene of battle because he had heard that his young son had been wounded there. The Doctor wanted to see if he could find him and do something for him. Fortunately the Doctor found the wounded boy in a farm house set up as a temporary hospital. He was able to do what he could, and his son's life was saved. This boy was the Oliver Wendell Holmes who was destined to become a distinguished justice of the Supreme Court.

Before returning to Boston Dr. Holmes, who was himself an amateur photographer, saw Brady's pictures.. Later he described his week on the battlefield in the *Atlantic Monthly*: "Let him who wishes to know what war is look at the series of illustrations. These wrecks of manhood thrown together in careless heaps or ranged in ghostly rows for burial were alive but yesterday. How dear to their little circles far away most of them!—how little cared for here by the tired party whose office is to consign them to earth! An officer, here and there, may be recognized; but for the rest—if enemies, they will be counted, and that is all. . . . It is so nearly like visiting the battlefields to look over these views, that all the emotions excited by the actual sight of the stained and sordid scene, strewn with rags and wrecks, come back to us. . . ." Dr. Holmes concluded, "The sight of these pictures is a commentary on civilization such as a savage might well triumph to show its missionaries."

To this very day Brady's pictures have remained a commentary on our civilization.

The life of a war photographer was not an easy one. He had to keep up with an army on the march. He had to make sure he had sufficient supplies with him. In cold weather his emulsion would be so sticky he had a hard time getting it to flow evenly over his glass plate. In hot weather it flowed quite readily, but then the plate had to be used almost at once or else it would spoil.

His picture told a story that was as good, if not better, than that of the war correspondent who had nothing to transport but a pencil and notebook. True, the newspaper man was exposed, but he could often see danger approaching and take cover. The photographer seated in his darkened wagon did not know what to expect nor from what direction it might come.

Many times Brady was under fire. Many times he lost part of his equipment. One of Brady's assistants, the very able Tim O'Sullivan, twice had his camera shattered by shells. On one occasion his dark cloth was torn by rifle fire and sand was scattered over his plates. But neither Brady nor O'Sullivan ever ran for cover. They carried on. They were courageous and dedicated men determined to capture history in its most agonizing moment.

As the War drew on year after year, there was a heavy financial drain on Brady. He wanted to operate like a big newspaper, but he did not have similar financial resources. As the theatre of war expanded, the drain grew heavier. To cover greater distances and follow the Union Army as the campaign stretched into the South, Brady built larger "What's-it Wagons," drawn by teams of horses and carrying more supplies, more food for the men, more fodder for the horses. Some of these larger wagons even had bunks for the operators so that they would have better shelter in cold or wet weather than they could find near the battlefields.

Because Brady's funds were running low and even though Anthony and Company continued to give him unlimited credit for supplies, Brady and his capable friend Alexander Gardner were forced to part. There is no record of any quarrel between these two gentle and kindly men. They remained friends. Gardner went off on his own and continued taking pictures of the war. Very probably Brady was unable to pay Gardner what he was worth. When they separated, Brady gave Gardner a duplicate set of his battlefield plates, probably in place of wages owed him. The plates had value. They could be used in place of currency.

During the War, the Washington gallery continued taking pictures of Lincoln, of members of his cabinet, of prominent statesmen and generals of the Army. Brady himself shuttled between the battlefield and Washington.

Throughout the war years, Brady and his wife Julia kept their apartment at the National Hotel. To maintain a crew of about 20 men on all the fronts of the war must certainly have been a drain. Says his biographer Horan, ". . . we know his own money, if not already exhausted, dwindled fast, yet we have no knowledge of the inner man. Was he discouraged, disheartened, embittered? And what of Julia, who waited for him patiently . . . ? Did she plead with him . . . to abandon this foolhardy venture before it destroyed them both? Did she write him tender, fearful letters and did he read them with a full heart by the light of campfire . . . ?"

Alas, these important questions cannot be answered. Not a single letter of Julia to Brady or of Brady to Julia has ever been located. Someday, perhaps, in an old trunk, in some dusty cabinet in a neglected attic such letters may be discovered. Then the past will become more real for us and we will know more of this man of history.

Chapter 13

Gettysburg and Peace

The full fury of battle in the Civil War came at Gettysburg, early in July, 1863. There on Pennsylvania's peaceful, rolling fields, hell itself boiled over. Brady and his men arrived in the fine summer weather to find a devil's bowl made in the wheat fields, a strange harvest of thousands of dead. In the silent aftermath of battle, the Blue of the North lay peacefully beside the Gray of the South.

Over 150,000 men took part in this violent action, and thousands upon thousands of cannon had blasted out their noisy destruction. Over a third of the men engaged were killed, wounded, or missing. For death and destruction, Gettysburg was the most violent battle, up to that time, in modern history. It shocked the whole world.

Beside Brady and his assistant Tim O'Sullivan,

Brady's old friend Gardner was also at Gettysburg. Much of the present-day record of this tragic moment in history we owe to these three able photographers. The most dramatic and unforgettable of all the Gettysburg pictures was O'Sullivan's "Harvest of Death." This picture of dead soldiers in a peaceful wheat field gave the nation a shocking insight into the reality of war. The picture cast a gloomy spell over the country. It was widely reproduced. It was perhaps the most emotionally disturbing picture taken during the entire War.

Lincoln saw "Harvest of Death" and was much moved by it. It filled his heart with a sadness he was unable to throw off. It has been said this picture inspired the famous Gettysburg Address, which he delivered on the battlefield in November of that year.

What else did these men record for posterity? They showed the wounded being carried away and some still waiting the return of the stretcher-bearers. They showed trees uprooted, orchards splintered, buildings in ruin, fences shattered, and the entire battleground, as far as the eye could see, dotted with fragments of blue and grey— pepper and salt. Hats, knapsacks, belts, rifles, canteens, coats removed because of the July heat and never picked up again. There were blankets and charred bits of uniforms, broken gun-carriage wheels and cannon that had exploded with the heat of overfiring. Here and there dead horses had fallen on dead men. More men, some only boys, attempting to climb over the dead horses, were killed and their bodies added to the pile.

All in all, what the photographers saw was appalling, shocking, grim. What they saw they recorded. And what they recorded can be seen today, a century after the actual event. Through these photographs Gettysburg will be known forever.

Gettysburg was the climax of the war. From then on General Ulysses S. Grant came into control. Battles followed one another in rapid succession. The lines stretched far from Washington. Brady put into operation his larger "What's-it Wagons," drawn by two horses.

Several times when President Lincoln came to the battlefields to consult with his generals, Brady was on hand to take pictures. Not many Presidents of the United States, before his day or since, ever visited the battlefield to consult with their generals.

After Sherman's March to the Sea through Georgia, the South's ability to make war was gradually destroyed. The cause of the South was lost. She fought nobly until nearly completely exhausted, then faced defeat. Grant's advantage over Lee lay in superior numbers and seemingly endless supplies. Grant pressed his advantage to the extreme. Richmond fell. Brady moved in while the shattered buildings were still smoldering and made a wonderful set of pictures.

Brady missed Lee's surrender to Grant at Appomattox because the photographer could not get there in time. He took some pictures of the house where the surrender had taken place several days after the historic event. But without the main actors of this drama, the building itself was an empty, almost meaningless shell.

Brady was determined to get some photographs of the distinguished and able commander of the Confederate forces, however, and so he journeyed back to Richmond and knocked boldly on the door of General Lee's home. His knock was answered by a servant. Brady told him he had come to see the General and wanted to take his picture. When Lee heard what Brady wanted, the General came out on the front porch and said, "It is utterly impossible, Mr. Brady. How can I sit for a photograph with the eyes of the world upon me as they are today?"

Lee's face was indeed traced with lines of care. The grief of defeat was plainly marked on him. But then Brady saw Mrs. Lee and a friend of the General's, Robert Ould. They both had known Brady before the outbreak of the War. Brady told them frankly how much he regretted having no record of the event that brought peace to the Union and how eager he was to make a likeness of the General.

The heartsick Lee listened in silence to the pleas of his wife and his friend. Finally he consented. He remained generous. He put on his uniform while Brady moved his camera around to the basement, below the back porch, for there the sunlight at this hour seemed best. Very soon Lee, together with his son in uniform and his aide, Colonel Walter Taylor, came out and sat for their pictures. Brady also took the General standing alone. In all he took six pictures. Each one remains today a beautiful example of his photographic art.

When the drums of war had been silenced and while the nation was still in anguish for so many dead, tragedy and a fresh sorrow struck its cruel blow. Five days after Lee's surrender, Lincoln was shot by an embittered Southerner, John Wilkes Booth. Lincoln died the following morning and the entire nation was plunged into grief.

From a rooftop close to his studio on Pennsylvania Avenue, Brady took a picture of Lincoln's funeral procession. Later he went to the Ford Theatre, where Lincoln had been shot, and took a photograph of the stage and one of the President's box, draped with the American flag that the spur of Booth's boot had torn as he leaped from the box to the stage.

With these pictures, a whole era ended for Brady. The wonderful backwoods lawyer was no more. The nation had lost its greatest President. Brady had lost a friend. The War was over. A whole era was over. A new one was ready to begin.

Chapter 14

The Weight of Time

While the nation was saved, Brady was ruined. He was not alone. Twelve tragic years, years of unrest and turmoil, followed the death of Lincoln.

These were years of stock swindles and currency manipulation that in 1869 caused a financial panic known as Black Friday to close the banks and create a depression over the entire land. Many people lost their homes and many were ruined beyond recovery. In the South the agony of reconstruction brought with it the carpet baggers—people from the North who came to exploit the South—and violence. Millionaires flourished and financial barons grew powerful on plundered wealth. Their greed knew no mercy, no humanity. But most of America was poor.

By 1869, the year of the Black Friday panic, Brady had lost almost everything he owned. To photograph the war, he had spent over $100,000 of his own money and besides this he had an equal amount in debts. He sold the four Central Park lots for $34,000 to pay off his most pressing debts.

Many galleries in Washington were ruined and forced to close. An advertisement in *Anthony's Photographic Journal* gives the full picture: "A Rare Chance. A gallery for sale. Well located for the past 20 years on Pennsylvania Avenue, Washington, D. C. Containing 15,000 valuable negatives of Distinguished Personages, filled with specimens, apparatus and everything requisite for a First Class Gallery. Price $1,500. Terms, $150 cash and $30 paid monthly will buy it, thus enabling the purchaser to pay for it from the proceeds of the business." There were many such advertisements. Photography, as well as other businesses, was on the rocks.

Profits from Brady's Washington gallery, which before the War had brought in an annual profit of $12,000, now fell to under $5,000. The demand for pictures had fallen off; photography was no longer a novelty.

The American public was so weary of war that they did not want to be reminded of such painful events as Brady's war views depicted with grim photographic reality. Pictures that Brady had thought would bring him a fortune were now a drug on the market. Those pictures, made at great expense, with much effort, and at the risk of life, were now unwanted. This situation was a most unexpected and great shock to Brady. Once he had been able to use his pictures as collateral to get credit. He had paid off Gardner with pictures. Brady could not understand the indifference of the public. He had no money, but he had 8,000 Civil War negatives. Wouldn't somebody buy them?

James Gordon Bennett's New York *Herald* said in 1866, in an editorial: "It would be extraordinary if Congress does not authorize the purchase of Mr. Brady's collection of historical works and locate them in some public place in the Capitol where all the world can study the progress of the Civil War in pages copied from life itself. We suppose the whole collection would not cost the government more than eighty or a hundred thousand dollars—a trifling sum—compared with their value as great historical works of art." This seemed like a good proposal: good for history, good for the nation, and good for Brady, but nothing came of it.

Brady's largest creditor was Anthony and Company, which had extended him unlimited supplies during all the years of the War. Since the Company was in the photographic supply business and since Brady and his men had taken everything in duplicate, the Company accepted Brady's duplicate set of plates in full payment of his debt.

Now once more, when the times were against it and all seemed impossible, Brady was able to use pictures in place of money.

Encouraged by this, Brady tried to dispose of his second set of negatives. He thought of selling them at auction to the highest bidder, and prepared a catalogue listing the important war scenes as well as the portraits of "distinguished men who figured in the early years of the present century . . . actors in the War with Mexico and portraits of eminent men and women of the whole century." This collection represented the work of 25 years.

The catalogue looked fine. But no buyer came forward.

Brady next tried to interest Congress in purchasing these plates. While Congress did not seem interested in the War, a report of the Library Committee in 1871 recommended the purchase of 2,000 portrait negatives of famous Americans. This prospect was very agreeable to Brady. He waited hopefully and patiently. But Congress took no action on this recommendation.

Finally Brady was forced to store all the boxes of plates in a warehouse. After the panic of 1873, one of the most serious that ever befell America, many people were ruined, and Brady was even worse off than before. He had sold his New York gallery and had only the Washington studio, which was having a hard time making ends meet. Storage bills on the plates piled up, and now because of hard times the warehouse company demanded payment. Brady could not meet it, and the storage company offered the Brady negatives for sale at public auction to satisfy its claim. At the auction on

July 31, 1874, the War Department paid the grand sum of $2,840 for all the plates. The storage company kept most of this money for its bill. The government seemed quite pleased with a good bargain. Brady made no complaint.

But somehow or other there seemed to be a fly in the ointment. About a year later General Ben Butler pointed out to Congress that Brady himself had not given a title to the government for these negatives. Did this property—the work of 25 years—really belong to the government or to Brady? This was a legal tangle. Was the title clear?

At this point, Congressman James A. Garfield, who later became President, proposed a bill in the House of Representatives with these words: "Here is a man who has given twenty-five years of his life (and the life of any man, however humble his station may be, is worth something considerable) to one great purpose—to preserving national monuments so far as photographic art can do so, with a view of making such a collection as nowhere exists in the world. . . . This man went so far as to send his organization into the field and some of his men were wounded in going near the battlefield to take pictures of the fight that was going on." To this speech before the House Garfield added a concluding bitter line: "The government should not take advantage of a man's distress."

Thus through the efforts of Garfield and General Butler an appropriation of $25,000 dollars was voted to

Brady in payment for the collection, which Garfield said was surely worth $150,000. So a full set of Bradys' pictures became the property of the government.

What happened to the plates? The War Department hardly understood the value of what it had. As Taft says: "The negatives were improperly and carelessly handled, loaned to individuals outside the War Department, not catalogued, and otherwise neglected for some years. As a result many were lost or broken and other scratched and cracked." When they were finally catalogued in 1897, the 8,000 plates had been reduced to a total of only 6,001.

The Great,
The Near-Great,
and The Unknown

PRESIDENT GRANT'S DAUGHTER NELLY
AND SON JESSE

GENERAL GEORGE ARMSTRONG CUSTER

Madame Catacazy

THE EDWIN MINER GALLAUDET FAMILY

PRESIDENT ULYSSES S. GRANT

AN UNKNOWN WASHINGTON BELLE

Chapter **15**

Nephew Levin Handy

B rady and his wife Julia, having no children of their own, took great pleasure in their nephew Levin Handy, who had been six years old when the Civil War broke out. He lived in Washington with his parents, and from his earliest childhood he was in and out of the gallery. Even as a baby, Levin knew the smell of the darkroom chemicals.

After the War, when the burden of hard times fell on Brady, still another worry came. Julia's health was not good. The years of war, worry about Mathew risking his life on the battlefield, mounting debts—all these things brought her health to a very low state. Against these dark clouds there was only one bright ray: young Levin.

One day, according to legend, three years after the War had ended, 12-year-old Levin came into the gallery and announced, "Uncle Mat, I have come to work for you. I want to be a photographer."

Brady laughed and said, "Levin, you are too young. Go back to school."

Levin told his uncle that the teacher had sent him home as a punishment for squirting water at a classmate. Levin was supposed to stay home until the teacher sent for him.

Brady told his nephew to go in the backroom and coat some plates. Brady was out of the studio the next day, but on the day after that he asked Levin why he was not in school. The teacher had not sent for him.

According to the legend the teacher forgot to send for Levin, and so he remained in his uncle's gallery. He did everything he could to make himself useful. He cleaned plates, he coated them, he mixed chemicals, and all the time he watched how his uncle worked. He studied the camera and saw how the shades over the skylights could be adjusted to vary the shadows on the face of the sitter.

Time and time again young Levin begged his uncle to allow him to work the camera. Brady, however, felt that the boy was not quite ready. But in two years he had taught young Levin all he knew of the secrets of photography. Then Levin was allowed to work behind the camera. Brady was happy to discover that Levin had a very fine talent for photography. He had a natural sense of composition and knew how to control the balance between the light and the dark.

In 1870, when Levin was 15 years old, he was a professional photographer taking pictures in Brady's famous gallery. He was, no doubt, at that time, the youngest professional photographer in the United States.

In 1872 photography took another great leap forward. An English physician, Richard Leach Maddox, freed photography from the awkwardness of the wet plate. His invention was announced to be "the driest of the dry processes." The wet plate used collodion to hold the sensitive silver salt, but the dry plate held the silver within a coating of gelatin.

As the English wet-plate process had been quick to displace the French daguerreotype process, so Maddox's dry plate promised to make the wet plate obsolete. No longer would a photographer be a slave to a process requiring him to prepare his plate in a darkroom a few minutes before he exposed his picture. A dry plate could be put away in a lightproof box and used even months after it had been coated. The dry plate was revolutionary.

Maddox himself hardly realized the importance of his discovery. He said that he did not find the wet process difficult or cumbersome. The only reason he had devised the dry plate was because he could not bear the nasty smell of ether in the hot greenhouse where he had his darkroom!

It took several years to perfect the dry plate, but

by 1879 a number of English firms were already supplying photographers with these new plates, which were now so fast and so sensitive that pictures at one twenty-fifth of a second were possible. This seemed most astonishing.

The photographic revolution in England soon spread across the Atlantic. In 1879, too, a young bank clerk in Rochester, New York, George Eastman, having read everything he could find on the new technique, began making dry plates. He was 25 years old. He sent some sample plates to Anthony and Company to see if they might be interested in marketing them. Anthony and Company agreed to take all the plates the young bank clerk could make in his spare time. They signed a contract for a full year.

Thus encouraged, Eastman decided to go into business seriously. He withdrew $3,000 from his savings, rented a room on the third floor of a building, and hired a helper. He still kept his job at the bank for another year, however, just to see how this new venture prospered.

In December, 1880, Anthony and Company advertised Eastman's dry plates for sale to the photographers of the United States. From this humble beginning arose a $1,000,000,000 business. A year or two later Eastman made his first flexible film. Then he designed a machine to coat glass plates and also film. Then came bromide paper and a camera that he gave a distinctive name to— a name now world famous—Kodak.

George Eastman in Rochester was one year older than young Levin Handy in Washington. The Eastman rise to fortune began with his association with Anthony and Company, founded by Brady's old friend, Edward Anthony.

But the Goddess of Fortune is fickle. Once she had led Brady to the great horizon of history. Now she had other favorites.

Brady was bankrupt. To add to his anguish, death took his beloved Julia on May 20, 1887. With her death he lost a good part of his courage. He was now 64 years old, his hair was grey, the fire in his lively eyes was gone, his little frame was bowed down. Brady gave up his apartment in the National Hotel; for it held too many memories of the past, a past of dignity, glory, recognition, and comfortable circumstances. He moved into a little bedroom in the home of his nephew Levin Handy.

Each day Brady walked to his gallery. He was a silent ruined man. But he was still proud. He carried the walking stick with its fine ivory handle that the Prince of Wales had once given him. In the dark mirror of his mind he saw the great pages of history on which he himself had been involved. What a long span! He had known people who had seen the founding fathers of the new nation. He had known Lincoln, Grant, and everyone of importance up to this very day. And now—how much longer? Who was left to record for posterity?

He seemed indifferent. He was tired. Part of the old spirited Brady was buried with his wife Julia. Part was buried in the history that engulfed him. "No one will ever know," he said, "what I went through in securing the negatives. The whole world can never appreciate it. It changed the whole course of my life. . . . Some of these negatives nearly cost me my life."

What had happened to the other set of plates that Brady gave to the Anthony Company in payment of his debt? Were these rare plates better cared for than those the Army had? In a way they were, but their history is also strangely checkered.

When pictures of the Civil War could no longer be sold to the public, the plates were stored away in boxes. Here fortunately they were not broken or scratched, nor loaned out to reckless people. They were just put away and forgotten.

Then some time later they were rediscovered by a man named John C. Taylor of Hartford, Connecticut. He went through the collection, made a few prints of what he liked, sold a few of the prints he made. Then Taylor disposed of the rest in the early 1880's exactly how or where is not known. Later two private collectors, Colonel Arnold A. Rand of Boston and General Albert Ordway of Washington, who knew the great historic value of Brady's work, managed to locate the plates and secure a clear title to the collection. They saw that the plates had been well protected and issued a catalogue. To this collection they added 2,000 more negatives, some by Brady and some by his assistants, by Alexander Gardner *and other famous photographers.

In time this valuable collection was offered to Congress, but no action was taken. For 20 years or more, the collection was completely forgotten. Then, in 1911, E. B. Eaton of Hartford, Connecticut, acquired possession of the plates and used them to publish a ten-volume work, *Photographic History of the Civil War*.

Most of these pictures came from the original plates Brady gave Anthony in payment of his debt. This photographic history of the war is today a most valuable reference work on the shelves of many libraries throughout the country.

Over the years Anthony and Company grew because photography again grew. For a long time the company was the largest photographic supply house in America. After several mergers with other companies, one of which was the Scovill Company, manufacturer of cameras, shutters and lenses, the name was changed to Ansco—An for Anthony and sco for Scoville.

Then by good fortune, in 1949 a man browsing around in his attic in the little town of Owego, New York, came upon an old box that had not been opened in years. There he discovered 44 fine Brady plates. How they got into this old attic no one could tell. The plates were in very fine condition and each was carefully wrapped in issues of the Washington *Evening Star*. Evidently they had been packed at two separate times for some of the newspapers had datelines of 1866 and some of 1874. Examination of the plates revealed that they were all made by Brady in his Washington studio after the end of the Civil War.

The Ansco Company, learning of this Brady find in Owego, New York, lost no time in purchasing the plates and giving them a safe haven.

So out of the dust of years, out of warehouses and old attics, Brady's work lives on. Often, in time, the long neglected and discarded is dusted off and shown in a place of honor.

Chapter 16

What, Brady Still Alive!

Brady and his nephew Levin Handy tried very hard to hang on to the Washington gallery and see if it could not be improved. They worked doggedly, but they barely managed to make ends meet.

Nevertheless, famous people knew the name Brady and occasionally came to the studio. During these years Brady added to his portrait gallery the pictures of Presidents James Garfield, Grover Cleveland, and William McKinley, and of such famous citizens as Thomas A. Edison, Andrew Carnegie, Mark Twain, and Walt Whitman. Just to round out the history of his years, he added some notable scenes of the time: Inaugural parades, views of the White House, and a photograph of the dedication of the Washington Monument, which took place on a cold February day in 1885.

His business, however, was not good. Brady was a forgotten man. He was tossed aside. One day, in the spring of 1891, George Alfred Townsend a well known reporter of the New York *World*, happened to be in Washington. As he was walking down the street he looked up and saw the name Brady on the sign of his gallery. Townsend stopped short. "What, Brady still alive!" he cried. "Brady, the Civil War photographer!"

He could not believe this possible and was certain that this Brady must be a relative or someone using the Brady name for his business. He climbed the stairs and later wrote that he found Brady, a "trim, wiry, square-shouldered figure with the light of an Irish shower-sun in his smile."

Yes, this was the real Brady—Brady of New York, Civil War Brady, the Brady who had photographed Lincoln and many others. Who could believe it?

Townsend's interview in the New York *World*, April 12, 1891, became an important document for those who would like to know and understand this modest little man who had in him the touch of greatness. There Brady spoke out about himself and his work.

The headline read: "Still Taking Pictures. Brady, the Grand Old Man of American Photography. Hard at work at sixty-seven. A Man Who Has Photographed More Prominent Men than any other Artist in the Country—Interesting Experiences with Well-Known Men of Other Days—Looking 'Pleasant.' "

Townsend had remembered Brady because some years earlier Brady had photographed him with his good friend Mark Twain. Now Brady told Townsend that Twain had come to the gallery only a few days before, and Brady had taken another picture of the writer, showing his great shock of white hair.

"What did he say?" asked Townsend.

Brady replied, "He looked over everything visible but of course not the unframed copies of my works and he said, 'Brady, if I was not tied up in my enterprises I would join you upon this material in which there is a fortune. . . . It would make the noblest subscription book of the age.'"

To this Brady said he replied, "From the first, I regard myself as under obligation to my country to preserve the faces of its historical men and women."

What happened to all the photographers who were trained by Brady? After the Civil War the men who had covered the various fronts in the Brady "What's-it Wagons" went off in different directions.

The very able and courageous Tim O'Sullivan joined a government geological exploration party and, in 1870, went through the Panama jungles on a surveying expedition. His camera helped the engineers find the best place for the canal to join the two oceans. He had many thrilling experiences and endured great hardships. From one exploring trip he and his party returned to Washington looking like bearded and starved savages, just bags of bones because of privation and exhaustion. After his health recovered, O'Sullivan worked in the field on map-making projects for the United States Army. In 1880 both Brady and Gardner recommended O'Sullivan for a job as photographer with the Treasury Department.

As for Alexander Gardner, who had parted from Brady even before the War ended, he closed his Washington gallery in 1867 and journeyed west to photograph the construction of the Union Pacific railroad. In the rough and tumble West of the early frontier days, Gardner created a most valuable collection of photographs of Indians, scouts, herds of buffalo, and cattle herds driven north from Texas, mining camps, the first beginnings of western towns, saloons, and the long moving trains of covered wagons bringing the American pioneer into new lands.

Besides O'Sullivan and Gardner, other men trained by Brady used the camera to record historical moments of the passing American scene. From Brady they had learned the lesson of history. So the spirit of Brady gave America the earliest pictures of the Great West and made many other valuable records of the time.

Chapter 17

Last Days

As the scope of photography advanced more and more, Brady's influence could be seen in everything that the camera was doing. Photography was now fully established and had become a vital part of American social life. Brady had done much to make it so.

By 1890, the dry plate had completely displaced the awkward wet-plate process. By this time Ansco and Eastman Kodak were already firmly established and thriving. New frontiers of photography were being explored. A small "detective" camera became a popular item and the forerunner of our modern school of miniature photography.

The idea of motion pictures was being investigated. Eadweard Muybridge had made a series of snapshots of a man walking and also of a horse running. The artist, Thomas Eakins, had made several series of pictures of a man walking, all on a single plate. These were among the earliest beginnings of the motion picture.

All this advancement Brady lived to see. He had been with photography at its very beginning. He had taken part in its growth and expansion. Now it was still making great strides forward. But alas! He himself was no longer part of this forward movement. Everything around him was advancing. He himself was declining.

To add to his unhappy condition, on April 16, 1895, as he was crossing the street in downtown Washington, he was struck down by a runaway horsecar. Unconscious and bleeding, he was rushed to the hospital where it was found that he had suffered severe lacerations and a broken leg. He had lost a good deal of blood and also had suffered internal injuries.

He was no longer young; a man over 70 does not recover very quickly from such a violent accident. He was a long time recuperating. He came out of the hospital on crutches. His eyesight, always poor, grew worse and worse; he was now forced to wear blue glasses to temper the harsh light of day. But soon he was able to walk without crutches and to hobble about with his favorite cane, the one presented to him by the Prince of Wales when he had been himself Prince of all Photographers in the world.

His courage was once more awakened. He now had

an idea in which he placed great hope. As soon as his health improved, he made plans to deliver a lecture in which he would tell his Civil War experiences and illustrate them with stereopticon slides of the famous scenes he had photographed. Thus he would himself bring history into the lecture hall.

To carry out this project, Brady insisted that he had to go to New York, for there would be the best place to launch his first lecture. His nephew Levin Handy and his wife did not like to have him going to New York all alone, but he convinced them that he had many old friends there. One in particular, William M. Riley, would look after him.

Before leaving Washington, Brady selected 128 pictures for his lecture, and Levin Handy agreed to make slides of them. Arriving in New York, Brady found a room in a house on East 10th Street, near his friend Riley and the site of his old 10th Street gallery. It was familiar ground, and there he felt at home. On 10th Street he had met Lincoln for the first time the day of the Cooper Union speech.

When Brady was settled in his rooming house, he began arranging his pictures in a logical order. For the few words of explanation he wanted to accompany each slide, he bought a pocket-size notebook and copied out the words in a clear hand.

A photograph of Brady's lecture book, reproduced in *Mr. Lincoln's Camera Man,* shows what Brady had in mind. For slide No. 46 he wrote: "Atlanta, Georgia, just after its capture. This is a view near the railroad depot in Atlanta just after the city was captured by General Sherman. Uncle Sam's baggage trains and the Boys in Blue are a strange sight to the inhabitants of Atlanta." These words seem sufficient, for the picture tells the rest of the story.

Sometimes Brady felt that he should give a fuller account of a historic event. For Slide No. 47, "Raising the Old Flag over Fort Sumter," Brady wrote, "April 14, 1865 (four years from the day the Rebels had compelled Major Anderson to haul down the Stars and Stripes from the flagstaff at Fort Sumter) Major General Anderson raises the same flag, now again in possession of the United States. The ceremony was of most intense interest. Charleston Harbor was filled with Uncle Sam's vessels covered with holiday flags. Great crowds thronged through Fort Sumter. Henry Ward Beecher delivered the oration. At a given signal, amid booming cannon and with bands playing, Major General Robert Anderson ran up the glorious old flag—and ran it up to stay, a perpetual menace to treason from within or foreign enemies from without. Long shall it wave."

The Seventh Regiment of New York made Brady an honorary member. He had been with the Regiment on so many fields of battle over so many years that they felt he was one of them. Many of the slides Brady selected for his lecture tour, which he hoped would include many of the main cities of the land, showed this distinguished

Seventh Regiment of New York in action.

So it was that the Seventh Regiment helped Brady engage Carnegie Hall for his first illustrated lecture on January 30, 1896. General Horace Porter, formerly on General Grant's staff, agreed to introduce Brady and serve as master of ceremonies. According to the custom of the day, besides the lecture there were also to be a reading of a patriotic poem and songs sung by a quartet. Such were the arrangements.

But there were difficulties. Brady thought that he could borrow a projector. But he wrote his nephew in Washington that he had searched all New York and Brooklyn without success. He had even advertised unsuccessfully in the *World* and two other papers. It would cost him $75 to have one made to order. "I see no other way," he wrote.

To get the money for the projector, Brady was forced to sell a portrait of himself painted years before. This money paid for the needed projector and perhaps gave him a little over to ease his desperate financial straits.

Meanwhile, his loyal friends were working on his behalf. William M. Riley sent out letters to prominent people asking them to sponsor Brady's lecture project. Many were proud to do so.

At the end of November, 1895, however, Brady was taken seriously ill with a kidney infection. He was very weak and confined to his bed in the 10th Street rooming house. Riley visited him daily to see that he had proper medical care and to do what he could. But no one could do much. Early in December Riley wrote Levin Handy in Washington that his uncle was "very weak and does not sit up at all, but I think is slowly mending."

This news was encouraging. Levin and his wife sent their uncle a small Christmas package from Washington. Brady was most grateful and asked his friend Riley to write and thank them for their kindness, for he was unable to write himself. Very soon afterwards, Riley was forced to write again to Washington. This time the news was not at all encouraging. Riley had taken Brady to the Presbyterian Hospital "and saw him comfortably quartered." Lack of money had forced Riley to place his old friend Brady in a charity ward, but he did not tell Levin Handy so; for Riley knew that Handy was having his own financial difficulties at this time.

In his letter of December 16th, Riley explained that he had moved Brady because in the hospital "he will have the most skillful attention and the very best of care." Riley assured Handy that he would visit his uncle every day and added that Levin should send letters to Brady in care of Riley.

It was a sad and lonely Christmas for a man who had been so active in the whirl of life, a man who was so understanding and friendly with both the great and the humble, the intimate of Lincoln and all the great of his day as well as of the Army drummer boys and hundreds of others during the long years. Now he was alone. The memories of the past and the solitude of the present were broken only by hospital routine.

This was the worst Christmas that Brady had ever known. But a spark of courage in him still glowed. He dreamed of his lecture series. He hoped that his health would improve and that enough strength would come back to let him to keep his engagement at Carnegie Hall at the end of January.

By the time the new year came, it was very evident that Brady's hopes were shattered. His strength did not return; on the contrary, he rapidly grew weaker. Riley, who visited him faithfully every day, knew then that recovery was impossible. Brady was dying. He sent a warning letter to Levin Handy.

The faithful Riley visited his friend for the last time on January 14. Riley never again saw his friend alive, for in the middle of the night Brady sank into a coma from which he never awoke. At 5:15 the next afternoon Brady died. Riley made arrangements to send his body to Washington so that it could be buried next to his beloved Julia in the Congressional Cemetery.

A final letter Riley sent to Brady's nephew was brought to light and printed by Meredith in his Mr. *Lincoln's Camera Man*. Riley wrote: "I have made a thorough examination of Mr. Brady's effects, and find no papers or other property that it would pay to send you. His wardrobe was only scant, and his coats in number, two. . . an overcoat and a frock coat which I gave away. The balance consists of some underwear, a few shirts and socks, etc., not of sufficient value to send, and so I thought

I would send them to the needy. There is an old worthless Waltham watch and also a ring. The latter you will, I suppose want, and if you would want, I will send to you."

The ring was the one the Prince of Wales had given him. And the old "worthless" watch was the one with which Brady had timed critical exposures for many thousands of his wonderful pictures.

A concluding line in this sad letter deepens the tragedy. "The satchel is old and broken," wrote Riley, "and one you would not want. The papers consist mainly of old and unimportant letters which I have put in the wastepaper basket. There are no other papers of the slightest value."

Here were the remains of a full life. A few rags given away to the needy. An old "worthless" watch. An old broken satchel. A few papers for the wastepaper basket. Are these the ashes and the final remains of a wonderful spirit?

No. This is only a dusty ash that the breeze of time blows away. Much more remains. There is another residue to life. Brady's pictures live.

Chapter 18

Of Time and of History

Levin Handy was in charge of the old Brady gallery in Washington and he was Brady's sole heir. After Brady's death all the plates in the studio, and they numbered thousands, as well as the old daguerreotypes, came into his possession.

Handy continued in Brady's tradition and in time, after he moved to Maryland Avenue, he changed the name of the gallery to the L. C. Handy Studios. By this name it was known to many people in Washington for many years.

Many famous people came to be photographed by Handy. Besides portraits, Handy specialized in copying important documents for the government. In fact, on his business card Levin Handy took pains to advertise himself as "The Accepted Photographer."

This was no idle boast. Handy did work for the Library of Congress, the State Department, the Department of Agriculture, and other branches of the government. He even had a dark room in the Library of Congress Building.

In 1903 the government in Washington had a bad scare. They had sent to the Jamestown Exposition some of the nation's most prized possessions, including the original Declaration of Independence, the original draft of the Constitution, Lincoln's famous Gettysburg Address, Washington's Farewell Address, and many other irreplaceable historical documents.

A fire broke out in the exhibition grounds at Jamestown, and only by good fortune were the flames checked before they reached the wooden building housing the priceless documents. As a result of this narrow escape, the Secretary of State ordered that in the future no valuable documents belonging to the government would be allowed to leave the Archives in Washington.

But how safe were the Archives? This question was not easy to answer. At length, after many official conferences, it was decided to have duplicate copies made of all the important documents in the possession of the government. This was a big job that would occupy a photographer for a number of years. Levin Handy was given the job. For three full years an armed guard delivered papers to Handy's studio and took away those documents he had already photographed. It was a long and painstaking task, but he completed it.

At Levin Handy's death, his studio was closed and the valuable collection of Brady-Handy plates were bequeathed to his two daughters, Mrs. Alice Cox and Mrs. Mary Evans. They had known their grand-uncle Mathew Brady when they were young and Brady lived in their home. But that was long ago. Still, their impressions were vivid and their memories clear.

They often told friends about their grand-uncle, recalling how he used to read the newspaper with a magnifying glass. They remembered him as quiet, modest, and soft spoken. He had often spoken of Lincoln and other important people he had known professionally.

Mrs. Evans and Mrs. Cox made the Brady-Handy plates available to historians and scholars. For years they maintained a small place of business and made duplicate prints from their plate collection for schools, colleges, historians, and publishers.

The original Brady plates which Congress bought long ago were finally transferred to the National Archives. Now they had a good home, were carefully stored and catalogued. In 1944 the Library of Congress added to this by buying the Eaton collection of Brady-Gardner plates which had been used to illustrate the ten-volume *History of the Civil War*.

Time has blown away the ash dust and revealed what was truly valuable.

Ten years after the Eaton collection was purchased by the government, the Library of Congress, in 1954, bought the Brady-Handy collection from Mrs. Cox and Mrs. Evans, who were now too old to make much use of the plates. For this collection they received $25,000.

At last Brady is not forgotten and his true value is appreciated. The plates are now in a place of safety. Some are small and some are fairly large, many 8 by 10 inches and even as large as 17 by 20 inches. Five of the plates now in the Library of Congress measure 19½ by 30 inches! Very few people, even in the world of photography, have ever seen a camera of this size. Yet, Brady must have had such a giant camera; otherwise these plates could never have been made.

The name Brady spells history. His whole life and his spirit are involved with history.

Brady's pictures of the Civil War give us an insight that no words could convey. History has been revised by many details revealed by Brady's pictures.

Many statesmen, poets, and other distinguished Americans are known mainly through Brady's photographs. Many of his photographs of the Presidents have been used for the engravings on bank notes and postage stamps.

When the question is asked, "What did Lincoln look like?" no one needs wonder. We know. Lincoln was photographed over 100 times. But half of these, and by far the best half, were made by Brady and Gardner. At least 35 of Lincoln's finest portraits were made by Brady. Through Brady we know Lincoln.

So it was that young Brady followed the golden wand of the Goddess of Fortune. He was involved with history and almost vanquished by it. Many moments on the battlefield with history were very dangerous. But Brady lived through them and carried on his work against all difficulties.

In the end he accomplished what he set out to do. He made the camera the eye of history, a faithful eye. And the record he left is full and rich. Few men have left a greater legacy. Through Brady the drama of war and the face of America in his lifetime live today.

NOTES ON THE PHOTOGRAPHS

From Brady's *The Gallery of Illustrious Americans.*—The portrait of Mathew Brady on Page 65 was taken in 1860, and is from the Ansco Historical Collection. The original is in the Brady Collection of the Library of Congress. All other photographs in this section are from the lithographs appearing in *The Gallery*. The oval portraits in the original measure 11 inches high by 9 inches wide in a frame 13-7/8 by 10-1/8 inches on a page 20-1/2 by 14-7/8 inches. The original pages were furnished by Mr. Manuel Kean of Kean Archives in Philadelphia, a pictorial collection on all subjects prior to 1890.

Prophets and a Prince.—The prophets on Page 99 are Harriet Beecher Stowe, author of *Uncle Tom's Cabin,* which did nothing to delay the coming of the Civil War that made Brady so famous; Lyman Beecher, her father, the most famous "hell fire and damnation" preacher of the first half of the 19th century; and her brother Henry Ward Beecher, the pride of the Plymouth Church of Brooklyn in the second half of the 19th century. The photograph here is from an Imperial in the Chicago Historical Society, the trimmed photograph proper being 18 inches high and 15 inches wide. All photographs from the Society were procured with the kind help of Mrs. Mary Frances Rhymer, Curator of Prints, and were copied with rare skill by Walter Krutz of the Society's Photographic

Laboratory. The studio portrait of Edward, Prince of Wales, and his entourage on Page 100 is also from one of the Society's Imperials, which has been retouched directly on the photograph. The original photograph proper is 13-1/4 inches high and 17-3/4 inches wide.

House Divided.—All photographs in this section except the view of the Brady "What's-it Wagon" and its crew in the field and the portraits of the Tom Thumb wedding party and of Mrs. John Slidell are from the Ansco Historical Collection at Binghamton, New York. Prints were obtained through the kind cooperation of Mr. Philip M. Mikoda, Manager of Sales Publicity for Ansco. The original of the Lincoln portrait on Page 115 is one of the approximately 35 portraits Brady made of Lincoln. This one was taken in 1863. The original is in the Library of Congress. The "What's-it Wagon" picture on Page 116 is from an original in the National Archives, reprinted by courtesy of the Signal Corps. The picture of Lincoln meeting with McClellan in the field was taken by Brady's partner, Alexander Gardner. The portrait of General Robert E. Lee on Page 117 is a copy of one of the six made by Brady shortly after Appomattox. The original is in the Library of Congress. The portrait of General Phil Sheridan, commander of the Union Army of the Shenandoah in 1864, taken after the War, is from one of the glass plates found in an attic in Owego, New York, in 1949, and now part of the Ansco Historical Collection. The picture on Page 119 of the dead lying behind the wall on Marye's Heights at Fredericksburg in May, 1863, is from an original in the National Archives. It is sometimes attributed to Brady, sometimes to his assistant Tim O'Sullivan, and sometimes to Captain A. J. Russell. Bystander Brady in the picture of General R. B. Potter and his staff on Page 120 is not an uncommon figure in the Brady Civil War pictures. The original is in the Library of Congress.

The photograph of Mrs. John Slidell on Page 121 was probably made in 1861, the year she and her husband left Washington to cast their lot with the Confederacy. The Chicago Historical Society Imperial from which it was taken is unretouched; the photograph is 19-1/2 inches high and 17-1/2 inches wide.

The picture of the Tom Thumb wedding party on Page 122 is reproduced from a carte de visite in the Chicago Historical Society. The carte de visite is 4 inches high by 2-1/2 inches wide. It is autographed on the back, which also bears notice that E. and H. T. Anthony, with whom Brady had a carte de visite contract, published it.

The Great, the Near-Great, and the Unknown.—All pictures in this section, Pages 157-162, are from the Ansco Historical Collection. The portrait of President Ulysses S. Grant's daughter Nelly and son Jesse is from one of the Oswego glass plates, as are also the other portraits. The portrait of Custer was made shortly before he left for the West to meet his end in the massacre that bears his name. Madame Catacazy, wife of the Russian minister in the 1870's, was a romantic figure in Washington, for she had run away from her first husband and had risked death before marrying her present one. Edward Miner Gallaudet was the youngest son of Thomas Hopkins Gallaudet, who in 1817 founded the first school for the deaf in the United States. The son established Gallaudet College at Washington in 1864 as the first U.S. institution for the higher education of the deaf.